LATIN FOR THE NEW MILLENNIUM

TEACHER'S MANUAL for Student Workbook

LEVEL 1

LATIN FOR THE NEW MILLENNIUM
Series Information

LEVEL ONE

Student Text (2008)

Student Workbook (2008)

College Exercise Book, Levels 1 and 2 (2012)

Teacher's Manual (2008)

Teacher's Manual for Student Workbook (2008)

ENRICHMENT TEXTS

From Romulus to Romulus Augustulus:
Roman History for the New Millennium (2008)

The Original Dysfunctional Family:
Basic Classical Mythology for the New Millennium (2008)

LEVEL TWO

Student Text (2009)

Student Workbook (2009)

Teacher's Manual (2009)

Teacher's Manual for Student Workbook (2009)

ENRICHMENT TEXTS

From Rome to Reformation:
Early European History for the New Millennium (2009)

The Clay-footed SuperHeroes:
Mythology Tales for the New Millennium (2009)

LEVEL THREE

Student Text (2012)

Teacher's Manual (2012)

ENRICHMENT TEXTS

Latin 3: Select Latin Enrichment Readings (2013)

ELECTRONIC RESOURCES

www.lnm.bolchazy.com

www.bolchazy.com/ebooks.htm

Quia Question Bank

LATIN FOR THE NEW MILLENNIUM

TEACHER'S MANUAL for Student Workbook

LEVEL 1

Milena Minkova and Terence Tunberg

Bolchazy-Carducci Publishers, Inc.
Mundelein, Illinois USA

Series Editor: LeaAnn A. Osburn
Volume Editors: Elisa C. Denja, LeaAnn A. Osburn
Contributing Editors: Timothy Beck, Donald E. Sprague, Vicki Wine
Cover Design & Typography: Adam Philip Velez
Cover Illustration: Roman Forum © Bettmann/CORBIS

Latin for the New Millennium
Teacher's Manual for Student Workbook, Level 1

Milena Minkova and Terence Tunberg

©2008 Bolchazy-Carducci Publishers, Inc.
All rights reserved

Bolchazy-Carducci Publishers, Inc.
1570 Baskin Road
Mundelein, Illinois 60060
www.bolchazy.com

Printed in the United States of America
2016
by CreateSpace

ISBN 978-0-86516-688-2

CONTENTS

PREFACE vi

CHAPTER 1 1

CHAPTER 2 4

CHAPTER 3 7

CHAPTER 4 12

CHAPTER 5 16

CHAPTER 6 21

CHAPTER 7 25

CHAPTER 8 30

CHAPTER 9 37

CHAPTER 10 42

CHAPTER 11 47

CHAPTER 12 52

CHAPTER 13 58

CHAPTER 14 64

CHAPTER 15 70

CHAPTER 16 78

CHAPTER 17 84

CHAPTER 18 90

CHAPTER 19 96

CHAPTER 20 103

CHAPTER 21 108

ENGLISH TO LATIN GLOSSARY 115

LATIN TO ENGLISH GLOSSARY 120

PHOTOGRAPHY CREDITS 127

PREFACE

This teacher's manual to the *Latin for the New Millennium* student workbook, level one, has been provided as a convenience for busy teachers.

In addition to containing the answers to all the questions in the student workbook, teachers may wish to take note of the various classical language learning standards that are addressed in the workbook.

STANDARD 1.1 STUDENTS READ, UNDERSTAND, AND INTERPRET LATIN

As well as numerous exercises in which students read Latin phrases and sentences, a number of reading passages are contained in the student workbook that are not in the student textbook. These Latin reading passages are based upon or adapted from Latin literature.

Chapter Three	Phaedrus' "Wolf and the Lamb"
Chapter Five	Letter from Terentia to Cicero
Chapter Six	About the Druids
Chapter Seven	Prose adaptations of Catullus' 3, 13, 49
Chapter Eight	Xerxes
Chapter Nine	About Jugurtha
	About Catiline
Chapter Ten	Prose adaptation of Vergil's Laocoön passage from *Aeneid*, 2
Chapter Twelve	Mucius Scaevola
Chapter Thirteen	Prose adaptations from Horace's *Odes* 2.7 & 3.7
Chapter Fifteen	Seneca and his Villa
	About the Habits of Senators
Chapter Sixteen	Selected adaptation from Pliny's "Ghost Story"
Chapter Seventeen	Selected adaptations from Suetonius' *Lives of Julius Caesar, Augustus, Tiberius, Caligula*
Chapter Eighteen	Selected adaptations from Petronius' *Satyricon*
Chapter Twenty	Selected adaptation from St. Augustine's *Confessions*
Chapter Twenty-one	Selected adaptation from Boethius' *Consolation of Philosophy*

STANDARD 1.2 STUDENTS USE ORALLY, LISTEN TO, AND WRITE LATIN

Every chapter provides exercises in which students write Latin. The teacher's manual for the level one textbook also includes exercises in which to use oral Latin.

Standards 2.1 and 2.2 which focus on the students' acquisition of knowledge about the culture of the Romans and Standards 3.1 and 3.2 that highlight making connections with other disciplines and expanding their knowledge are all met through the reading of the culturally and linguistically authentic material contained in this workbook. In the student textbook you will find the material to meet Standards 4.1 and 4.2 which center around making comparisons between the ancient and modern world.

 When you see this icon, you will know that some additional information is being given only in this teacher manual and it is not included in the student workbook.

With its variety of exercises, reinforcement of vocabulary and grammar, and content questions relevant to each chapter, the workbook will provide additional support in consolidating the material presented in the student text.

CHAPTER 1

▶ EXERCISE 1

Identify the part of speech of the word in bold in each sentence. The Reading Vocabulary may be consulted.

1. Rhēa Silvia **fīliōs** amat. — noun
2. Amūlius Rōmulum et Remum **in** aquam pōnit. — preposition
3. Mars Rhēam Silviam **amat**. — verb
4. Agricola **fīliōs** cūrat. — noun
5. Lupa Rōmulum et Remum **bene** cūrat. — adverb
6. Nauta aquam **et** terram amat. — conjunction

Mars, god of war and father of Romulus and Remus.

▶ EXERCISE 2

Identify whether the word in bold is the subject, predicate nominative, or direct object in each sentence. The Reading Vocabulary may be consulted. (The word *nōn* means "not.")

1. Amūlius nōn est **deus**. — predicate nominative
2. Puella **Rōmam** amat. — direct object
3. **Lupa** fīliōs cūrat. — subject
4. Nauta **aquam** amat. — direct object
5. **Rōmulus et Remus** Rōmam aedificant. — subject
6. **Āthlēta** ambulat. — subject

· 1 ·

▶ EXERCISE 3

Decline the following noun.

1. *aqua, aquae*, f.

	Singular	Plural
Nominative	aqua	aquae
Genitive	aquae	aquārum
Dative	aquae	aquīs
Accusative	aquam	aquās
Ablative	aquā	aquīs

▶ EXERCISE 4

Identify the case and number of the following nouns. For some, more than one answer is possible. Translate each form into English.

Example: terrae
genitive singular   of the land   dative singular   to/for the land   nominative plural   the lands

1. nautārum — genitive plural: of the sailors, sailors'
2. fīliae — genitive singular: of the daughter; dative singular: to/for the daughter; nominative plural, the daughters
3. terram — accusative singular: the land
4. agricolīs — dative plural: to/for the farmers; ablative plural: by/with the farmers
5. poētās — accusative plural: the poets
6. lupa — nominative singular: the she-wolf
7. Rōmā — ablative singular: by/with/from Rome
8. āthlētae — genitive singular: of the athlete; dative singular: to/for the athlete; nominative plural: the athletes

▶ EXERCISE 5

Identify the case and number of the following nouns. Change the singular forms into plural and the plural forms into singular. For some, more than one answer is possible.

Example: puellā
ablative singular   puellīs

1. puellae — genitive singular, dative singular, nominative plural; puellārum/puellīs/puella
2. puella — nominative singular; puellae
3. puellās — accusative plural; puellam
4. puellārum — genitive plural; puellae
5. puellīs — dative plural, ablative plural; puellae/puellā
6. puellam — accusative singular; puellās

▶ EXERCISE 6

Complete the following sentences by consulting the Latin reading passage and Reading Vocabulary. Make your answers grammatically correct.

Example: Mārs __Rhēam Silviam__ amat.

1. Rhēa Silvia __filiōs / Rōmulum et Remum__ amat.
2. Amūlius __Rhēam Silviam / Rōmulum et Remum__ nōn (*not*) amat.
3. Rhēa Silvia __filiōs / Rōmulum et Remum__ cūrat.
4. Amūlius __Rhēam Silviam / Rōmulum et Remum__ nōn (*not*) cūrat.
5. Lupa __ad aquam__ ambulat.
6. Lupa __Rōmulum et Remum__ amat.
7. Lupa __Rōmulum et Remum__ bene cūrat.

Ancient coin showing Romulus and Remus with the she-wolf.

CONTENT QUESTIONS

After completing Chapter 1, answer these questions.

1. Who were the founders of Rome?
   Romulus and Remus.

2. Name the eight parts of speech.
   Noun, pronoun, adjective, verb, adverb, conjunction, preposition, interjection.

3. What three properties does every noun have?
   Every noun has case, number, and gender.

4. List the names of the five cases in order.
   Nominative, genitive, dative, accusative, ablative.

5. What is the usual gender of nouns of the first declension?
   Feminine.

CHAPTER 2

▶ EXERCISE 1
Fill in the blanks by writing **1** for first conjugation and **2** for second conjugation verbs.

1. habitō, habitāre, habitāvī, habitātum   _1_
2. habeō, habēre, habuī, habitum   _2_
3. vocō, vocāre, vocāvī, vocātum   _1_
4. teneō, tenēre, tenuī, tentum   _2_
5. amō, amāre, amāvī, amātum   _1_
6. parō, parāre, parāvī, parātum   _1_

▶ EXERCISE 2
Fill in the blanks with the missing Latin personal ending or English pronoun.

	Singular Latin	Singular English	Plural Latin	Plural English
First person	-o or -m	I	-mus	we
Second person	-s	you	-tis	you
Third person	-t	s/he/it	-nt	they

▶ EXERCISE 3
Conjugate in the present tense.

1. *vocō, vocāre, vocāvī, vocātum*

	Singular	Plural
First person	vocō	vocāmus
Second person	vocās	vocātis
Third person	vocat	vocant

2. *dēbeō, dēbēre, dēbuī, dēbitum*

	Singular	Plural
First person	dēbeō	dēbēmus
Second person	dēbēs	dēbētis
Third person	dēbet	dēbent

▶ EXERCISE 4

Identify the person and number of each verb and give three English translations for each.

Example: vocās
second singular   you call, do call, are calling

1. amant   third plural: they love, do love, are loving
2. habēs   second singular: you have, do have, are having
3. tenet   third singular: s/he/it holds, does hold, is holding
4. ambulāmus   first plural: we walk, do walk, are walking
5. dēbētis   second plural: you owe, do owe, are owing/you ought/must/should
6. cūrant   third plural: they care for (take care of); do care for (take care of); are caring for (taking care of)

▶ EXERCISE 5

Fill in the blanks with the correct form of the words in parentheses.

Example:
Fīliī fābulam ___amant___. (amāre)

1. Poētae fābulās ___parant___. (parāre)
2. Puella fōrmam ___cūrat___. (cūrāre)
3. Nautae aquam ___amant___. (amāre)
4. Puellae lupam ___vident___. (vidēre)

A sketch of an ancient actor wearing the mask of comedy.

▶ EXERCISE 6

Translate into Latin.

1. You are telling stories! — Fābulās nārrās!
2. We call the poet. — Poētam vocāmus.
3. She takes care of the daughter. — Fīliam cūrat.
4. You (plural) ought to care for the fatherland. — Patriam cūrāre dēbētis.
5. I love Rome. — Rōmam amō.
6. They expect the sailors. — Nautās exspectant.

CONTENT QUESTIONS

After completing Chapter 2, answer these questions.

1. Which two major Latin authors from prior to 100 BCE are discussed in Chapter 2?
   Plautus and Terence.

2. What models did Plautus follow in his work?
   Greek comedy.

3. In which principal part is the stem of the verb found? How is the stem found?
   In the second principal part; by removing the *-re* from the infinitive.

4. How do you distinguish the first from the second conjugation?
   The first conjugation has a characteristic vowel *-ā*, while the second has a characteristic vowel *-ē*.

5. In what respect do the subject and the verb agree?
   In number.

Roman theatre in Mérida, Spain where a modern day summer festival devoted to production of ancient plays is held annually. Mérida was founded in 25 BCE and its original name was Emerita Augusta from which the modern name of Mérida is derived.

CHAPTER 3

▶ EXERCISE 1
Decline the following nouns.

1. *servus, servī*, m.

	Singular	Plural
Nominative	servus	servī
Genitive	servī	servōrum
Dative	servō	servīs
Accusative	servum	servōs
Ablative	servō	servīs
Vocative	serve	servī

2. *magister, magistrī*, m.

	Singular	Plural
Nominative	magister	magistrī
Genitive	magistrī	magistrōrum
Dative	magistrō	magistrīs
Accusative	magistrum	magistrōs
Ablative	magistrō	magistrīs
Vocative	magister	magistrī

▶ EXERCISE 2
Translate into Latin.

1. in the stream — in rīvō
2. with the sons — cum fīliīs
3. in the mind — in animō
4. on the roads — in viīs
5. with the friend — cum amīcō
6. in the water — in aquā

▶ EXERCISE 3

In the sentences below, use an appropriate noun from the first sentence to fill in the blank with a noun in the vocative case. Then translate both sentences.

Example: Poēta fābulam parat. Exspectāmus, ___poēta___, fābulam.
The poet is preparing a story.   We are waiting for the story, poet.

1. Puer lupam timet. Nōn dēbēs, ___puer___, lupam timēre.
   The boy fears the she-wolf. Boy, you ought not to fear the she-wolf.

2. Fīlius domī nōn est. Tē, ___fīlī___, exspectāmus.
   tē – you (accusative)
   The son is not at home. Son, we are waiting for you.

3. Vir amīcum vocat. Amīcus, ___vir___, nōn est domī.
   The man is calling his friend. Man, (your) friend is not at home.

4. Amīcus animum bonum nōn habet. Dēbēs, ___amīce___, animum bonum habēre.
   bonum – good (accusative singular masculine)
   The friend does not have a good spirit. Friend, you ought to have a good spirit.

5. Puella in agrīs ambulat. Tē, ___puella___, domī exspectāmus.
   tē – you (accusative)
   The girl is walking in the fields. Girl, we are waiting for you at home.

Modern actors in ancient garb.

▶ EXERCISE 4
Translate into Latin.

1. The sons do not expect Demea.
   Dēmea, Dēmeae, m.

   Fīliī Dēmeam nōn exspectant.

2. Syrus does not fear Demea.
   Syrus, Syrī, m.

   Syrus Dēmeam nōn timet.

3. The sons ought not to live in the fields.

   Fīliī in agrīs habitāre nōn dēbent.

4. The sons walk on the roads with friends.

   Fīliī in viīs cum amīcīs ambulant.

▶ EXERCISE 5
Translate this fable into English.

Phaedrus, a Roman author who lived during the first half of the first century CE, was a freed slave of the emperor Augustus. He wrote the first collection of fables in Latin literature that has come down to us. Phaedrus follows the plots of his Greek predecessor Aesop, but puts them in a poetic form. The fable below is adapted from the original.

Lupus et agnus in rīvō stant. Lupus superior stat et agnus īnferior. Lupus agnum vocat: "Aquam, agne, turbās."
Agnus lupum timet: "Ego, lupe, īnferior stō. Aquam nōn turbō."
Lupus: "Tē (*accusative of* tū) nōn amō."
Lupus agnum dēvorat.

The wolf and the lamb stand in the stream. The wolf stands higher and the lamb lower.

The wolf calls the lamb: "Lamb, you muddy the water."

The lamb fears the wolf: "Wolf, I stand lower. I do not muddy the water."

Wolf: "I do not like you."

The wolf devours the lamb.

agnus, agnī, m. – lamb
dēvorō, dēvorāre, dēvorāvī, dēvorātum – to devour
īnferior – lower (downstream)
lupus, lupī, m. – wolf

stō, stāre, stetī, statum – to stand
superior – higher (upstream)
turbō, turbāre, turbāvī, turbātum – to muddy, to stir up
   (compare "turbulence")

▶ EXERCISE 6

Using the Reading Vocabulary from Exercise 5, fill in the blanks with the appropriate endings.

Example: Agnus nōn est in agr __ō__.

1. Agn __us__ est in rīv __ō__.
2. Agnus lup __um__ nōn vocat.
3. Agnus aqu __am__ nōn turbat.
4. Lupus agn __um__ nōn amat.
5. Nōn dēbēs, lup __e__, agnum dēvorāre.
6. Dēbēs, agn __e__, lupum timēre.

The wolf and lamb face each other.

CONTENT QUESTIONS

After completing Chapter 3, answer these questions.

1. Why have Terence's comedies remained popular?
   Because of the universal moral problems in them.

2. When is the vocative case used?
   Used to address someone.

3. In what declension and what noun-type is the vocative different from the nominative? What is the ending?
   Second declension, nouns in *–us*. The ending is *–e*.
   Second declension, nouns in *–ius*. The ending is *–ī*.

4. With what word do we usually translate the genitive? With what mark of punctuation can the genitive also be translated?
   "Of." The apostrophe.

5. What is a prepositional phrase?
   A preposition with a noun in a certain case.

A sketch of an ancient mask of comedy.

Teacher's Manual • Chapter 3 • 11

CHAPTER 4

▶ EXERCISE 1

Decline the following nouns.

1. *praemium, praemiī*, n.

	Singular	Plural
Nominative	praemium	praemia
Genitive	praemiī	praemiōrum
Dative	praemiō	praemiīs
Accusative	praemium	praemia
Ablative	praemiō	praemiīs
Vocative	praemium	praemia

2. *vinculum, vinculī*, m.

	Singular	Plural
Nominative	vinculum	vincula
Genitive	vinculī	vinculōrum
Dative	vinculō	vinculīs
Accusative	vinculum	vincula
Ablative	vinculō	vinculīs
Vocative	vinculum	vincula

Armed Roman soldiers.

▶ EXERCISE 2

Translate into Latin.

1. I give the reward to the famous man.
   Praemium virō praeclārō dō.

2. We tell the story about the treachery to the sons.
   Fābulam dē dolō fīliīs nārrāmus.

3. They prepare the camp for the armed men.
   Castra virīs armātīs parant.

4. We show (mōnstrāmus) the road to the Romans.
   Viam Rōmānīs mōnstrāmus.

5. You (plural) prepare chains for bad men.
   Vincula virīs malīs parātis.

6. We do not give poison to men.
   Venēnum virīs nōn damus.

▶ EXERCISE 3

Change the noun-adjective pairs into the singular if they are plural and into plural if they are singular. For some, more than one answer is possible.

Example: virō malō
virīs malīs

1. amīcī iūstī — amīcōrum iūstōrum/amīcus iūstus
2. bellōrum māgnōrum — bellī māgnī
3. rīvō māgnō — rīvīs māgnīs
4. agrī māgnī — agrōrum māgnōrum/ager māgnus
5. poētam iūstum — poētās iūstōs
6. āthlēta praeclārus — āthlētae praeclārī

▶ EXERCISE 4

Translate into Latin. The Reading Vocabulary in Chapter 4 may be consulted.

1. Pyrrhus wants to have land in Italy.
   Pyrrhus terram in Ītaliā habēre vult.

2. A deserter walks into the camp of the Romans.
   Profuga in castra Rōmānōrum ambulat.

3. They ought not to give the bad man a large reward.
   Nōn dēbent virō malō māgnum praemium dare.

4. Fabricius wants to have victory through legitimate war.
   Fābricius bellō iūstō victōriam habēre vult.

5. Fabricius orders armed men to walk with the deserter to the camp of Pyrrhus.
   Fābricius iubet virōs armātōs cum profugā ad Pyrrhī castra ambulāre.

▶ EXERCISE 5

Change the noun to the correct case required by the prepositions in parentheses and then translate.

Example: vir (cum)
cum virō   with the man

1. fīlia (cum) — cum fīliā: with the daughter
2. viae (in + accusative) — in viās: into the roads
3. aqua (ad) — ad aquam: to/toward the water
4. aqua (in + ablative) — in aquā: in/on the water
5. castra (ad) — ad castra: to/toward the camp
6. casae (ē) — ē casīs: out of the houses
7. nautae (cum) — cum nautīs: with the sailors

▶ EXERCISE 6

Fill in the blanks with the correct form of the adjective in parentheses and translate each sentence. The Reading Vocabulary in Chapter 4 may be consulted.

Example: Profuga est ___malus___. (malus)
The deserter is bad.

1. Pyrrhus est rēx ___praeclārus___. (praeclārus)
   Pyrrhus is a famous king.

2. Pyrrhus ___māgnam___ terram in Ītaliā habēre vult. (māgnus)
   Pyrrhus wants to have big land in Italy.

3. Virī __armātī/armātum__ profugam vident. (armātus)
   Armed men see the deserter. / Men see the armed deserter.

4. Fābricius victōriam __iūstam__ vult. (iūstus)
   Fabricius does want a legitimate victory.

5. Fābricius virōs __Rōmānōs__ vocat. (Rōmānus)
   Fabricius calls the Roman men.

6. Fābricius profugae __vīnctō__ praemium nōn dat. (vīnctus)
   Fabricius does not give a reward to the tied deserter.

Roman leg armor.

CONTENT QUESTIONS

After completing Chapter 4, answer these questions.

1. In what genre of literature did Cicero excel?
   Oratory, among other genres.

2. What is the main topic in Cicero's treatise *Dē officiīs* (On duties)?
   The relationship between what is morally right (*honestum*), and what is expedient (*ūtile*).

3. In what way do the neuter nouns of the second declension decline differently from the masculine nouns of the second declension?
   The nominative and accusative singular are the same: also the nominative and accusative plural end in *-a*.

4. What is the case of the indirect object?
   Dative.

5. What is the basic rule for how adjectives must agree with nouns?
   They must agree in case, number, and gender.

CHAPTER 5

▶ EXERCISE 1

Conjugate in the passive voice, including the passive infinitives. Translate each form.

1. *exspectō, exspectāre, exspectāvī, exspectātum*
2. *iubeō, iubēre, iussī, iussum*

	passive form of *exspectō* + English translation	passive form of *iubeō* + English translation
First person singular	exspector	iubeor
	I am being expected	I am being ordered
Second person singular	exspectāris	iubēris
	you are being expected	you are being ordered
Third person singular	exspectātur	iubētur
	s/he/it being expected	s/he/it is being ordered
First person plural	exspectāmur	iubēmur
	we are being expected	we are being ordered
Second person plural	exspectāminī	iubēminī
	you are being expected	you are being ordered
Third person plural	exspectantur	iubentur
	they are being expected	they are being ordered
Infinitive	exspectārī	iubērī
	to be expected	to be ordered

The Kansas state seal reads, *Ad Astra Per Aspera*, "To the stars through difficulties (rough things)."

▶ EXERCISE 2

Decline the following adjectives.

1. *asper, aspera, asperum*

Singular

	Masculine	Feminine	Neuter
Nominative	asper	aspera	asperum
Genitive	asperī	asperae	asperī
Dative	asperō	asperae	asperō
Accusative	asperum	asperam	asperum
Ablative	asperō	asperā	asperō
Vocative	asper	aspera	asperum

Plural

	Masculine	Feminine	Neuter
Nominative	asperī	asperae	aspera
Genitive	asperōrum	asperārum	asperōrum
Dative	asperīs	asperīs	asperīs
Accusative	asperōs	asperās	aspera
Ablative	asperīs	asperīs	asperīs
Vocative	asperī	asperae	aspera

2. *crēber, crēbra, crēbrum*

Singular

	Masculine	Feminine	Neuter
Nominative	crēber	crēbra	crēbrum
Genitive	crēbrī	crēbrae	crēbrī
Dative	crēbrō	crēbrae	crēbrō
Accusative	crēbrum	crēbram	crēbrum
Ablative	crēbrō	crēbrā	crēbrō
Vocative	crēber	crēbra	crēbrum

Plural

	Masculine	Feminine	Neuter
Nominative	crēbrī	crēbrae	crēbra
Genitive	crēbrōrum	crēbrārum	crēbrōrum
Dative	crēbrīs	crēbrīs	crēbrīs
Accusative	crēbrōs	crēbrās	crēbra
Ablative	crēbrīs	crēbrīs	crēbrīs
Vocative	crēbrī	crēbrae	crēbra

▶ EXERCISE 3

Keeping the same case, number, and gender replace the adjective with the one in parentheses. Translate the changed phrase. For some more than one answer is possible.

Example: praeclāram fēminam (miser)
miseram fēminam   wretched woman

1. bonās fīliās (pulcher) _pulchrās fīliās: beautiful daughters_
2. bonōrum agricolārum (miser) _miserōrum agricolārum: of the wretched farmers_
3. malīs armīs (miser) _miserīs armīs: to/for the wretched weapons; by/with/from the wretched weapons_
4. bonae fēminae (pulcher) _pulchrae fēminae: of the beautiful woman; to/for the beautiful woman; beautiful women_
5. praeclārōs virōs (miser) _miserōs virōs: wretched men_
6. iūstō animō (miser) _miserō animō: to/for the wretched soul; by/with/from the wretched soul_

▶ EXERCISE 4

Change the infinitives in parentheses to the verb form required to complete the sentence. Translate each sentence.

Example: Auxilium ā bonō virō _datur_. (dare)
Help is being given by the good man.

1. Venēna ā malīs virīs et fēminīs _parantur_. (parāre)
   Poisons are being prepared by bad men and women.
2. Auxilium ab amīcīs _datur_. (dare)
   Help is being given by friends.
3. Terra ā nautīs nōn _vidētur_. (vidēre)
   The land is not seen by the sailors.
4. Castra ā virīs armātīs _tenentur_. (tenēre)
   The camp is being held by armed men.
5. Nauta ā familiā _exspectātur_. (exspectāre)
   The sailor is expected by the family.
6. Patria ā puerīs et puellīs _amātur_. (amāre)
   The country is loved by the boys and girls.

▶ EXERCISE 5

Fill in the blanks with the correct form of the adjectives and translate each sentence. The Reading Vocabulary may be consulted.

Example:
Casa nōn est _____māgna_____. (māgnus)
The cottage is not big.

1. Animus Cicerōnis (*of Cicero*) est _____miser_____. (miser)
   Cicero's mind is sad.

2. Terentia nōn est _____misera_____. (miser)
   Terentia is not wretched.

3. Fīlia Terentiae est valdē _____pulchra_____ et fīlius Terentiae est valdē _____pulcher_____. (pulcher)
   The daughter of Terentia is very beautiful and the son of Terentia is very handsome.

4. Praemia _____pulchra_____ exspectō. (pulcher)
   I expect beautiful rewards.

5. Fābula ā _____pulchrā_____ fēminā nārrātur. (pulcher)
   The story is being told by a beautiful woman.

6. Virō _____miserō_____ auxilium dare dēbēmus. (miser)
   We ought to give help to the wretched man.

Statue of a Roman woman holding a baby, just as Cicero's wife Terentia must have held their daughter Tullia at one time.

▶ EXERCISE 6

Translate the following passage. The Reading Vocabulary may be consulted.

Terentia Cicerōnī (*to Cicero*) salūtem plūrimam dīcit.

Epistula tua, Cicero, ā mē (*me*) tenētur. Sī dolēs, doleō. Nōn sōlum tamen cōnsilia mala ā malīs virīs contrā tē parantur, sed etiam auxilium māgnum ā bonīs virīs parātur. Itaque nōn dēbēmus dolēre. Nam familia nostra (*our*) nōn est misera. Epistulae tuae longae ā mē, ā fīliō, ā pulchrā fīliā exspectantur. Valē!

Terentia is greeting Cicero. (Literally it means "[s/he] says [i.e., wishes] very much health [the best of health] to …")

Your letter, Cicero, is held by me. If you feel pain, I feel pain. However, not only bad plans are being designed by bad men against you, but also great help is being prepared by good men. And so we ought not to feel pain. For our family is not wretched. Your long letters are expected by me, by (our) son, by (our) beautiful daughter. Goodbye!

CONTENT QUESTIONS

After completing Chapter 5, answer these questions.

1. What is the difference between the active and passive voices?
   In the active voice the subject of the verb performs the action, while in the passive voice the subject receives the action.

2. Where was Cicero when he wrote sad letters to his family?
   Cicero was in exile in Greece, sent there by his political enemies.

3. What construction is used with the passive voice to indicate the person who performs the action?
   Ablative of agent preceded by the preposition *ā* (*ab*).

4. What spelling difference distinguishes the declension of *pulcher* and *miser*?
   Pulcher loses the *-e* in its declension, while *miser* keeps it.

5. When is the preposition *ab* used instead of *ā*?
   Ab is used before vowels.

CHAPTER 6

▶ EXERCISE 1

Write the corresponding forms of *possum* and translate both verb forms.

1. sunt — (they) are/there are — possunt — (they) are able
2. es — (you) are — potes — (you) are able
3. sumus — (we) are — possumus — (we) are able
4. est — (s/he/it) is/there is — potest — (s/he/it) is able
5. sum — (I) am — possum — (I) am able
6. estis — (you <pl.>) are — potestis — (you <pl.>) are able

▶ EXERCISE 2

Translate into English.

1. Timēre nōn dēbēmus.
   We ought not to fear.

2. Amārī dēbētis.
   You ought to be loved.

3. Ambulāre solēmus.
   We are accustomed to walk.

4. Cūrārī dēbēs.
   You ought to be cared for.

5. In viā esse dēbeō.
   I ought to be on the road.

6. In agrō esse nōn solēmus.
   We are not accustomed to be in the field.

7. Dē cōnsiliīs cōgitāre dēbent.
   They ought to think about the plans.

▶ EXERCISE 3
Translate into Latin.

1. I am able to walk.
   Possum ambulāre.

2. I am used to being loved.
   Soleō amārī.

3. Poets cannot always be just.
   Poētae nōn semper iūstī esse possunt.

4. They are not used to preparing plans.
   Cōnsilia parāre nōn solent.

5. Rewards ought to be given to the athletes.
   Praemia āthlētīs darī dēbent.

6. We are not used to remaining in the darkness.
   Manēre in tenebrīs nōn solēmus.

▶ EXERCISE 4
List the transitive and intransitive verbs in this modified reading passage. The Reading Vocabulary may be consulted.

Inter Gallōs sunt virī māgnī quī vocantur Druidēs. Sacra Gallōrum ā Druidibus cūrantur. Druidēs ā Gallīs valdē timentur: nam auctōritātem māgnam habent, et dē virīs bonīs et malīs iūdicant. Praemia et poenae ā Druidibus dantur. Vīta Gallōrum ā Druidibus cūrātur. Propter Druidum scientiam māgnam multī puerī ad Druidēs ambulant et cum Druidibus diū manent. Druidēs puerōs docent. Druidēs dē sacrīs scientiam māgnam habent, sed librōs et litterās nōn amant. Nam sacra sunt māgna, sī in tenebrīs iacent. Itaque sacra Gallōrum nōn litterīs, sed memoriā servantur. Druidēs scientiam māgnam memoriā servant. Itaque dum Druidēs exempla docent et fābulās nārrant, puerī memoriam firmant.

Transitive
vocantur, cūrantur, timentur, habent, iūdicant, dantur, cūrātur, docent, amant, servantur, servant, nārrant, firmant

Intransitive
sunt, ambulant, manent, iacent

This relief from the second century CE shows a teacher with students. This image, found in the area of the Roman site *Noviomagus Trēvirōrum*, is frequently cited as evidence for Roman schooling. In Roman times and still today, the area, modern-day Neumagen, is celebrated for its wine production. Today the relief is housed in the Rheinisches Landes Museum in Trier, Germany.

▶ EXERCISE 5

Change the following sentences into the passive voice. The Reading Vocabulary may be consulted.

Example: Puer puellam exspectat.
Puella ā puerō exspectātur.

1. Virī māgnī praemia dant. — Praemia ā virīs māgnīs dantur.
2. Druidēs puerōs docent. — Puerī ā Druidibus docentur.
3. Gallī librōs et litterās nōn amant. — Librī et litterae ā Gallīs nōn amantur.
4. Puerī memoriam firmant. — Memoria ā puerīs firmātur.

▶ EXERCISE 6

Change the following sentences into the active voice. The Reading Vocabulary may be consulted.

Example: Puella ā puerō exspectātur.
Puer puellam exspectat.

1. Sacra Gallōrum ā Druidibus cūrantur. — Druidēs sacra Gallōrum cūrant.
2. Virī māgnī ā Gallīs timentur. — Gallī virōs māgnōs timent.
3. Vīta Gallōrum ā virīs māgnīs cūrātur. — Virī māgnī vītam Gallōrum cūrant.
4. Sacra ā Gallīs servantur. — Gallī sacra servant.

Here the face of Julius Caesar depicts his worries, cares, and concerns.

CONTENT QUESTIONS

After completing Chapter 6, answer these questions.

1. Which are Caesar's principal works?
   "On the Gallic War" and "On the Civil War."

2. What happened on the Ides of March 44 BCE?
   Caesar was murdered by his enemies.

3. Who were the Druids?
   High priests and ruling class in Gaul at the time of Caesar.

4. How are the verbs *sum* and *possum* similar in conjugation?
   The verb *possum* is actually composed of *sum* added to the prefix *pot-*.

5. What is the difference between transitive and intransitive verbs?
   Transitive verbs have direct objects and intransitive ones do not.

6. What is a complementary infinitive?
   A complementary infinitive completes the meaning of certain verbs.

CHAPTER 7

▶ EXERCISE 1
Decline the following phrases.

1. *longa pāx*

	Singular	Plural
Nominative	longa pāx	longae pācēs
Genitive	longae pācis	longārum pācum
Dative	longae pācī	longīs pācibus
Accusative	longam pācem	longās pācēs
Ablative	longā pāce	longīs pācibus
Vocative	longa pāx	longae pācēs

2. *miser amor*

	Singular	Plural
Nominative	miser amor	miserī amōrēs
Genitive	miserī amōris	miserōrum amōrum
Dative	miserō amōrī	miserīs amōribus
Accusative	miserum amōrem	miserōs amōrēs
Ablative	miserō amōre	miserīs amōribus
Vocative	miser amor	miserī amōrēs

▶ EXERCISE 2
Translate into Latin.

1. to/for the sisters — sorōribus
2. to/for the old man — senī
3. by means of love — amōre
4. I love the sister. — Sorōrem amō.
5. joy of peace — gaudium pācis
6. words of the old men — verba senum

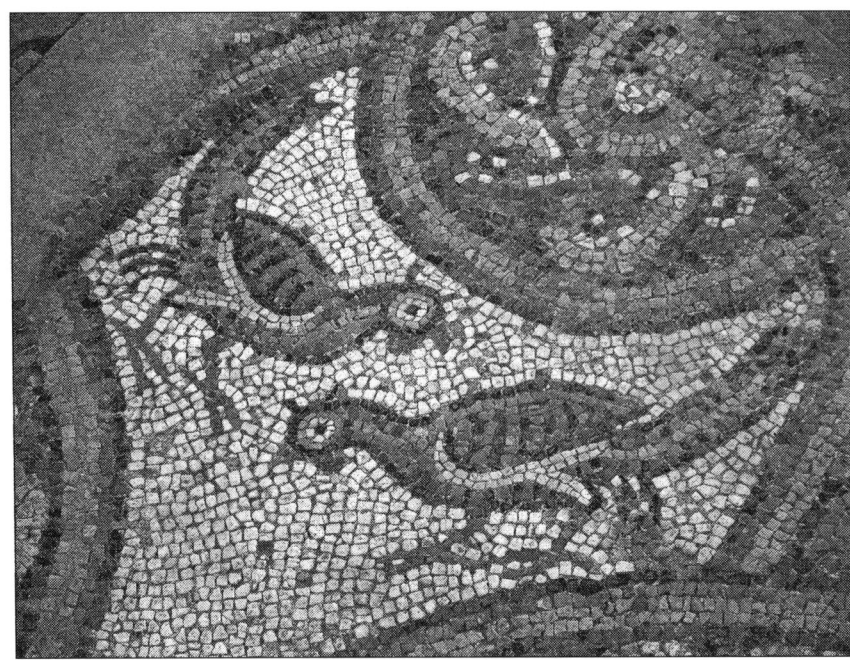
Mosaic of pheasants.

▶ EXERCISE 3

Change the following direct statements into indirect statements using the accusative and infinitive construction.

Example: Passer manet in gremiō dominae.
Poēta videt _passerem manēre in gremiō dominae._

1. Passer est dēliciae puellae.

   Poēta putat _passerem esse dēliciās puellae._

2. Catullus verba senum ūnīus assis aestimat.

   Catullus nārrat _sē verba senum ūnīus assis aestimāre._

3. Māgna praemia āthlētae dantur.

   Poēta videt _māgna praemia āthlētae darī._

4. Cicerō epistulās longās exspectat.

   Cicerō putat _sē epistulās longās exspectāre._

5. Druidēs librōs et litterās nōn amant.
   Druidēs, Druidum, m. pl. – Druids

   Caesar nārrat _Druidēs librōs et litterās nōn amāre._

▶ EXERCISE 4

In one of his poems, Catullus tells about the death of his girl's sparrow. Translate into English the following adaptation of this story.

Passer puellae est mortuus. Puella dē passere valdē dolet. Multae lacrimae sunt in oculīs puellae. Nam puella putat sē amīcum bonum nunc nōn habēre. Passer in tenebrīs ambulat. Passer ad puellam nunc ambulāre nōn potest et in gremiō puellae tenērī nōn potest. Catullus nārrat sē quoque dē passere dolēre. Nam putat oculōs puellae esse turgidōs.

The sparrow of the girl is dead. The girl really grieves about the sparrow. There are many tears in the eyes of the girl. For the girl thinks that now she does not have a good friend. The sparrow is walking in the shadows. The sparrow cannot walk to the girl and cannot be held on the girl's lap. Catullus tells that he is also hurting (mourning) about the sparrow. For he thinks that the eyes of the girl are swollen.

mortuus, mortua, mortuum – dead
quoque – also
turgidus, turgida, turgidum – swollen

 **This passage is an adaptation of Catullus 3.**

▶ EXERCISE 5

In this poem, some believe that Catullus is mocking Cicero. Translate the following adaptation of this poem into English. Then change all the sentences into indirect statements by beginning with *Catullus nārrat*.

Ego sum valdē malus poēta et Cicerō est valdē bonus ōrātor. Verba Cicerōnis sunt semper pulchra. Cicerōnem tamen ūnīus assis aestimāre soleō.

Cicerō, Cicerōnis, m. – Cicero
ōrātor, ōrātōris, m. – orator

Translation: I am a very bad poet and Cicero is a very good orator.
Indirect Statement: Catullus nārrat sē esse valdē malum poētam et Cicerōnem valdē bonum ōrātōrem.

Translation: Cicero's words are always nice.
Indirect Statement: Catullus nārrat verba Cicerōnis esse semper pulchra.

Translation: I, however, am not accustomed to care a bit for Cicero.
Indirect Statement: Catullus nārrat sē Cicerōnem tamen ūnīus assis aestimāre solēre.

 **Teachers should note Catullus' irony or sarcasm in this adaptation of Catullus 49: according to some, he apparently says the reverse of what he actually means in the first sentence.**

The typical number of nine diners on three couches is shown in this drawing of Romans at a dinner party.

▶ EXERCISE 6

In one of his poems, Catullus sends a dinner invitation to his friend, but it turns out to be quite a surprising invitation. Translate into English.

Dēbēs ambulāre ad casam meam, Fabulle, et cēnāre mēcum. Putō nōs posse bonam cēnam habēre. Sed dēbēs multum cibum portāre. Nam Catullus pecūniam nōn habet et nōn putat sē posse cēnam parāre. Sed Catullus potest Fabullō mūnera pulchra dare. Itaque Catullus et puella Fabullum exspectant.

You have to walk to my cottage, Fabullus, and dine with me. I think that we can have a good dinner. But you have to bring lots of food. For Catullus does not have money and does not think that he can prepare a dinner. But Catullus can give to Fabullus nice gifts. And so Catullus and the girl are expecting Fabullus.

cēna, cēnae, f. – dinner
cēnō, cēnāre, cēnāvī, cēnātum – to dine
cibus, cibī, m. – food
Fabullus, Fabullī, m. – Fabullus
mēcum – with me

mūnera (accusative plural) – gifts
nōs (accusative) – we
pecūnia, pecūniae, f. – money
portō, portāre, portāvī, portātum – to carry

 **This passage is an adaptation of Catullus 13.**

28 • Latin for the New Millennium

CONTENT QUESTIONS

After completing Chapter 7, answer these questions.

1. To what group of poets did Catullus belong?
   Neoterics, or new poets.

2. What trend in Latin literature did Catullus start?
   Catullus started the trend of love elegy.

3. With what word did Catullus and the elegiac poets after him typically describe the woman they adored?
   Domina or mistress.

4. What is characteristic of the nominative singular of the nouns of the third declension?
   It follows no regular pattern of formation.

5. What kinds of verbs introduce an indirect statement?
   Verbs of saying, thinking, and observing.

6. With what conjunction is the indirect statement usually translated in English?
   With the conjunction "that."

CHAPTER 8

▶ EXERCISE 1

Conjugate the following verb in the active and passive voice. Give the active and passive infinitives.

1. dēcernō, dēcernere, dēcrēvī, dēcrētum

Active

	Singular	Plural
Infinitive	dēcernere	
First person	dēcernō	dēcernimus
Second person	dēcernis	dēcernitis
Third person	dēcernit	dēcernunt

Passive

	Singular	Plural
Infinitive	dēcernī	
First person	dēcernor	dēcernimur
Second person	dēcerneris	dēcerniminī
Third person	dēcernitur	dēcernuntur

▶ EXERCISE 2

Translate into Latin.

1. we are being conquered — vincimur
2. to be understood — intellegī
3. it is said — dīcitur
4. you (plural) are being sought — petiminī
5. they understand — intellegunt
6. we say — dīcimus

Xerxes with his servants.

▶ EXERCISE 3

Translate the following questions. Then choose the best answer for each and translate. The Reading Vocabulary may be consulted.

1. Quōmodo (*in what way*) Xerxēs bellum contrā Graecōs parāre dīcitur?

    Xerxēs bellum contrā Graecōs in Graeciā parāre dīcitur.

    Xerxēs bellum contrā Graecōs in nāvibus parāre dīcitur.

    Xerxēs bellum contrā Graecōs cum māgnā industriā parāre dīcitur.

    In what way is Xerxes said to prepare (for) war against the Greeks?

    Xerxēs bellum contrā Graecōs cum māgnā industriā parāre dīcitur.

    Xerxes is said to prepare (for) war against the Greeks with great care.

2. Quō īnstrumentō (*by what instrument/means*) Graecī Persās vincunt?

   Graecī in Graeciā Persās vincunt.

   Graecī cum dolō Persās vincunt.

   Graecī mūrīs ligneīs Persās vincunt.

   By what instrument/means are the Greeks conquering the Persians?

   Graecī mūrīs ligneīs Persās vincunt.

   The Greeks are conquering the Persians with wooden walls.

3. Quōmodo (*in what way*) Graecī Persās vincunt?

   Graecī in terrā Persās vincunt.

   Graecī Persās māgnā fortitūdine vincunt.

   Graecī in nāvibus Persās vincunt.

   In what way are the Greeks conquering the Persians?

   Graecī Persās māgnā fortitūdine vincunt.

   The Greeks are conquering the Persians with great courage.

4. Ē quā rē (*from what thing*) Athēniēnsēs līberantur?

   Athēniēnsēs timōre līberantur.

   Athēniēnsēs fortitūdine līberantur.

   Athēniēnsēs mūrīs ligneīs līberantur.

   From what thing are the Athenians freed?

   Athēniēnsēs timōre līberantur.

   The Athenians are freed from fear.

5. Cūius reī auxiliō (*by the help of what thing*) Themistoclēs Graecōs servat?

   Themistoclēs Graecōs in templō Delphicō servat.

   Themistoclēs Graecōs in bellō servat.

   Themistoclēs Graecōs cōnsiliīs bonīs servat.

   By the help of what thing is Themistocles saving the Greeks?

   Themistoclēs Graecōs cōnsiliīs bonīs servat.

   Themistocles is saving the Greeks through his good plans.

▶ EXERCISE 4

Translate the following sentences, then make each one passive. The subject of the active sentence will become an ablative in the passive sentence. The Reading Vocabulary may be consulted.

Example: Cōnsilia bona Graecōs servant.
Good plans are saving the Greeks.
Graecī cōnsiliīs bonīs servantur.

Themistoclēs Graecōs servat.
Themistocles is saving the Greeks.
Graecī ā Themistocle servantur.

1. Athēniēnsēs cōnsilia Themistoclis intellegunt.
   The Athenians understand the plans of Themistocles.
   Cōnsilia Themistoclis ab Athēniēnsibus intelleguntur.

2. Persae cum multīs mīlitibus Graecōs petunt.
   The Persians are rushing at the Greeks with many soldiers.
   Graecī ā Persīs cum multīs mīlitibus petuntur.

3. Pȳthia ōrācula dīcit.
   The Pythian priestess is saying (uttering) oracles.
   Ōrācula ā Pȳthiā dīcuntur.

4. Bona cōnsilia Graecōs līberant.
   Good plans are freeing the Greeks.
   Graecī bonīs cōnsiliīs līberantur.

5. Athēniēnsēs Persās in nāvibus vincunt.
   The Athenians defeat the Persians in ships.
   Persae ab Athēniēnsibus in nāvibus vincuntur.

6. Dux māgnus Athēniēnsēs timōre līberat.
   A great leader is freeing the Athenians from fear.
   Athēniēnsēs timōre ā duce māgnō līberantur.

7. Mūrī ligneī Athēniēnsēs servant.
   Wooden walls save the Athenians.
   Athēniēnsēs mūrīs ligneīs servantur.

► EXERCISE 5

Fill in the blanks with the appropriate ablative from the list below and translate each sentence. The Reading Vocabulary may be consulted.

    litterīs   terrā   bellō   Pȳthiā   mīlitibus   templō

1. __Bellō__ līberārī et in pāce vīvere dēbēmus.
   We ought to be freed from war and live in peace.

2. Graecī ā __mīlitibus__ Persārum petuntur.
   The Greeks are being rushed at by the soldiers of the Persians.

3. Ōrācula ā __Pȳthiā__ dantur.
   The oracles are given by the Pythian priestess.

4. Cōnsilium hominum bonōrum __litterīs__ servātur.
   Advice of good men is preserved by literature.

5. Themistoclēs cōnsilia Apollinis in __templō__ exspectat.
   Themistocles awaits the counsels of Apollo in the temple.

6. Athēniēnsēs ā __terrā__ nāvigant et nāvēs Persārum petunt.
   The Athenians sail away from land and seek the ships of the Persians.

A view of the front of the Treasury in Delphi, Greece. Like many other cities, Athens built a treasury along the sacred path that winds its way up toward the Temple of Apollo, home of the famous Delphic Oracle. The treasury would have housed the many lavish gifts dedicated to Apollo by the city in return for the god's oracular advice. These offerings can be seen today in the Delphi Museum. The building is partly reconstructed and the white pieces are not original.

▶ EXERCISE 6

Translate the following passage into English.

The passage below is loosely based on the work of the Greek historian Herodotus (fifth century BCE) who wrote about the Persian Wars. Although Herodotus is called "The Father of History," his narrative is by no means always historically accurate.

Xerxēs est dux multōrum mīlitum. Dum mīlitēs Xerxis aquam ex rīvō bibunt, rīvus siccātur. Mīlitēs Xerxis Hellespontum trānsīre dēbent. Xerxēs dēcernit sē et virōs armātōs Hellespontum pontibus transīre posse. Mīlitēs pontēs aedificant. Tunc mare procellā turbātur et pontēs servārī nōn possunt. Xerxēs putat mare esse malum. Itaque iubet mare verberārī. Mīlitēs Xerxis mare verberant.

Xerxes is the leader of many soldiers. While the soldiers of Xerxes drink water from a river, the river is dried out.

The soldiers of Xerxes have to cross the Hellespont. Xerxes decides that he and the armed men can cross the

Hellespont with bridges. The soldiers build bridges. Then the sea is stirred up by a storm and the bridges cannot be saved.

Xerxes thinks that the sea is bad. And so he orders the sea to be whipped. The soldiers of Xerxes whip the sea.

aedificō, aedificāre, aedificāvī, aedificātum – to build
bibō, bibere, ——, —— – to drink
Hellespontus, Hellespontī, m. – the Hellespont, a strait between Europe and Asia
mare, maris, n. – sea
pōns, pontis, m. – bridge

procella, procellae, f. – storm
siccō, siccāre, siccāvī, siccātum – to make dry
trānsīre – to cross
turbō, turbāre, turbāvī, turbātum – to stir up
verberō, verberāre, verberāvī, verberātum – to flog, beat, whip
Xerxēs, Xerxis, m. – Xerxes

CONTENT QUESTIONS

After completing Chapter 8, answer these questions.

1. What sort of works did Cornelius Nepos write?
   Biographies of famous Greeks and some Romans.

2. When did Themistocles live and what was his main achievement?
   In the fifth century BCE. Themistocles prepared a successful strategy with which the Greeks defeated the Persians in a naval battle.

3. When may the ablative of manner be accompanied by a preposition?
   When the noun is modified by an adjective.

4. What distinguishes the third conjugation infinitive from the second conjugation infinitive?
   The short -*e* in the stem.

5. With what case is the idea of separation expressed in Latin?
   With the ablative.

6. Which form of the third conjugation is quite different from the other conjugations?
   The present passive infinitive ending in -*ī*.

CHAPTER 9

▶ EXERCISE 1

Conjugate the following verb in the active and passive voice. Give the active and passive infinitives.

1. *sciō, scīre, scīvī, scītum*

Active

	Singular	Plural
Infinitive	scīre	
First person	sciō	scīmus
Second person	scīs	scītis
Third person	scit	sciunt

Passive

	Singular	Plural
Infinitive	scīrī	
First person	scior	scīmur
Second person	scīris	scīminī
Third person	scītur	sciuntur

▶ EXERCISE 2

Decline the following phrases.

1. *pulchrum corpus*

	Singular	Plural
Nominative	pulchrum corpus	pulchra corpora
Genitive	pulchrī corporis	pulchrōrum corporum
Dative	pulchrō corporī	pulchrīs corporibus
Accusative	pulchrum corpus	pulchra corpora
Ablative	pulchrō corpore	pulchrīs corporibus
Vocative	pulchrum corpus	pulchra corpora

2. *mala mors*

	Singular	**Plural**
Nominative	mala mors	malae mortēs
Genitive	malae mortis	malārum mortium
Dative	malae mortī	malīs mortibus
Accusative	malam mortem	malās mortēs
Ablative	malā morte	malīs mortibus
Vocative	mala mors	malae mortēs

3. *bonum exemplar*

	Singular	**Plural**
Nominative	bonum exemplar	bona exemplāria
Genitive	bonī exemplāris	bonōrum exemplārium
Dative	bonō exemplārī	bonīs exemplāribus
Accusative	bonum exemplar	bona exemplāria
Ablative	bonō exemplārī	bonīs exemplāribus
Vocative	bonum exemplar	bona exemplāria

▶ EXERCISE 3

Translate into English.

1. sentiunt — they feel
2. audiuntur — they are being heard
3. marium — of the seas
4. venīs — you are coming
5. audīminī — you (plural) are being heard
6. urbium — of the cities
7. scīris — you are being known
8. audīrī — to be heard
9. venītis — you (plural) are coming
10. cīve — by/with the citizen
11. animālium — of the animals
12. corporī — to/for the body

▶ EXERCISE 4

Translate into Latin.

1. in the sea — in marī
2. many examples — multa exemplāria
3. You (plural) are coming to the cities. — Ad urbēs venītis.
4. to the sea — ad mare
5. The times are not good. — Tempora nōn sunt bona.
6. We save (our) bodies. — Corpora servāmus.
7. Joy is being felt. — Gaudium sentītur.
8. (He) behaves well. — Bene sē gerit.
9. We hear the speech. — Ōrātiōnem audīmus.
10. You know the deception. — Dolum scīs.
11. The women do not believe. — Mulierēs nōn crēdunt.

▶ EXERCISE 5

Translate the following text into Latin.

Catiline has great courage in body and in spirit. However, the spirit of Catiline is bad and he loves bad examples. For the leader has in his mind the death of Roman citizens. Catiline knows that he does not seek peace, but seeks war. Catiline decides to conquer the Romans, but is conquered by the consul. The head of Catiline is being carried from a battle to the city.

Catilīna māgnam fortitūdinem in corpore et in animō habet. Animus tamen Catilīnae est malus et mala exemplāria amat. Nam dux in animō habet mortem cīvium Rōmānōrum. Catilīna scit sē nōn petere pācem, sed bellum. Catilīna dēcernit Rōmānōs vincere, sed ā cōnsule vincitur. Caput Catilīnae ē pugnā ad urbem portātur.

Catilīna, Catilīnae, m. – Catiline
portō, portāre, portāvī, portātum – to carry
pugna, pugnae, f. – battle

It was during the lifetime of King Jugurtha of Numidia (160–104 BCE) that this Republican denarius from 136 BCE was minted. The coin shows the helmeted head of the personification of Roma.

▶ EXERCISE 6

Translate the following text into English.

Iugurtha māgnum rēgnum in Africā habēre dēcernit et auxilium ā virīs Rōmānīs petit. Iugurtha pecūniam virīs Rōmānīs dat. Itaque Iugurtha sentit sē posse ex pecūniā multās rēs habēre. Iugurtha dīcit urbem Rōmam vēndī posse. Propter hoc Iugurtha putat mortem ad urbem venīre posse.

Jugurtha decides to have a great kingdom in Africa, and he seeks help from Roman men. Jugurtha gives money

to Roman men. And so Jugurtha feels that he can have many things from money. Jugurtha says that the city of Rome

can be sold. Because of this Jugurtha thinks that death can come to the city.

Africā, Africae, f. – Africa
hoc – this
Iugurtha, Iugurthae, m. – Jugurtha
pecūnia, pecūniae, f. – money

rēgnum, rēgnī, n. – kingdom
rēs (accusative plural) – things
vēndō, vēndere, vēndidī, vēnditum – to sell

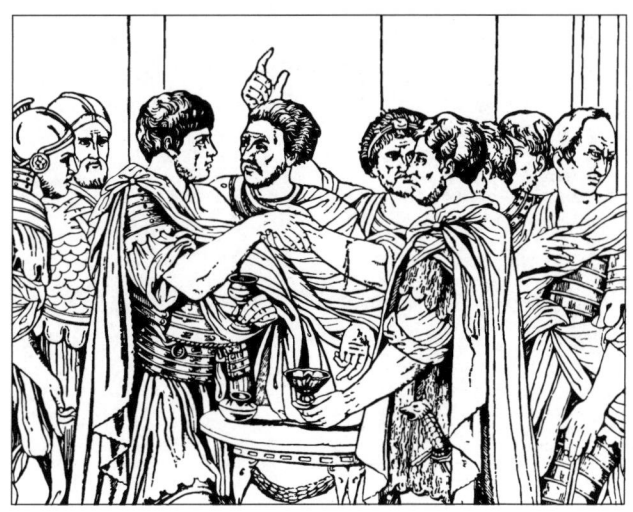

Soldiers during the time of the Catilinarian conspiracy
that eventually failed.

CONTENT QUESTIONS

After completing Chapter 9, answer these questions.

1. Where is there a slight irregularity in the fourth conjugation present?
   There is an additional *-u* in the third person plural active and passive.

2. In which cases are the *i*-stems different from the other words belonging to the third declension?
   In the ablative singular neuter; in the genitive plural; in the nominative, accusative, and vocative plural neuter.

3. In what way are the *-ar, -al* and *-e* nouns different from the other *i*-stems of the third declension?
   Their ablative ending is *-ī*, not *-e*.

4. What is the peculiarity of neuter nouns shared by all declensions?
   The nominative, accusative, and the vocative of all the neuter nouns are the same; furthermore, the ending for the nominative, accusative, and vocative plural is *-a*.

5. Who was the first great Roman historian writing in Latin whose works survive?
   Sallust.

6. Who was Catiline?
   A bankrupt politician who conspired to overthrow the Roman republic.

CHAPTER 10

▶ EXERCISE 1

Conjugate the following verb in the active and passive voice. Give the active and passive infinitive.

1. *iaciō, iacere, iēcī, iactum*

Active

Infinitive: iacere

	Singular	Plural
First person	iaciō	iacimus
Second person	iacis	iacitis
Third person	iacit	iaciunt

Passive

Infinitive: iacī

	Singular	Plural
First person	iacior	iacimur
Second person	iaceris	iaciminī
Third person	iacitur	iaciuntur

▶ EXERCISE 2

Decline the following phrases.

1. *hostis ācer*

	Singular	Plural
Nominative	hostis ācer	hostēs ācrēs
Genitive	hostis ācris	hostium ācrium
Dative	hostī ācrī	hostibus ācribus
Accusative	hostem ācrem	hostēs ācrēs
Ablative	hoste ācrī	hostibus ācribus
Vocative	hostis ācer	hostēs ācrēs

2. *dux fēlīx*

	Singular	Plural
Nominative	dux fēlīx	ducēs fēlīcēs
Genitive	ducis fēlīcis	ducum fēlīcium
Dative	ducī fēlīcī	ducibus fēlīcibus
Accusative	ducem fēlīcem	ducēs fēlīcēs
Ablative	duce fēlīcī	ducibus fēlīcibus
Vocative	dux fēlīx	ducēs fēlīcēs

3. *dōnum celebre*

	Singular	Plural
Nominative	dōnum celebre	dōna celebria
Genitive	dōnī celebris	dōnōrum celebrium
Dative	dōnō celebrī	dōnīs celebribus
Accusative	dōnum celebre	dōna celebria
Ablative	dōnō celebrī	dōnīs celebribus
Vocative	dōnum celebre	dōna celebria

▶ EXERCISE 3

Translate into English.

1. bona — good things / a good woman
2. fēlīcēs — fortunate people
3. cupiuntur — they are desired / sought after
4. capior — I am captured
5. puellārum fēlīcium — of the fortunate girls
6. hostibus fortibus — to/for the brave enemies / by/with the brave enemies
7. iūsta — a just woman / just things
8. fugiunt — they flee
9. mīlitum ācrium — of the fierce soldiers
10. cōnsulis celebris — of the renowned consul

EXERCISE 4

Translate into Latin.

1. to/for the renowned temple — templō celebrī
2. Fortunate people have many things. — Fēlīcēs multa habent.
3. You (plural) think about the fierce soldiers. — Dē mīlitibus ācribus cōgitātis.
4. of the renowned city — urbis celebris
5. Just people do not think about rewards. — Iūstī de praemiīs nōn cōgitant.
6. Gifts are desired. — Dōna cupiuntur.
7. Bad things are not always seen. — Mala nōn semper videntur.
8. The fortunate do not fear. — Fēlīcēs nōn timent.
9. to/for the fierce enemy — hostī ācrī

Laocoön and his two sons being strangled by serpents from the sea.

▶ EXERCISE 5

Translate the following passage into English.

Lāocoōn Trōiānus cōnsilia hostium intellegit. Equum ligneum ante portam urbis positum videt. In equō esse perīculum māgnum scit. Trōiānōs dē perīculō monēre cupit. Trōiānī autem dē perīculō scīre nōn cupiunt. Equum esse dōnum pulchrum crēdunt. Itaque verba Lāocoontis nōn audiunt. Minerva Trōiānōs ōdit et Trōiam dēlēre cupit. Minerva Trōiānōs dē perīculō monērī nōn cupit. Itaque serpentēs māgnās in terram mittit. Serpentēs ācrēs Lāocoontem et fīliōs occīdunt.

Laocoön, the Trojan, understands the enemies' plans. He sees the wooden horse placed before the gate of the city. He knows that there is a great danger in the horse. He wants to warn the Trojans about the danger. But the Trojans do not want to know about the danger. They believe that the horse is a beautiful gift. Therefore they do not hear the words of Laocoön. Minerva hates the Trojans and wants to destroy Troy. Minerva does not want the Trojans to be warned about the danger. So she sends great serpents onto the land. The fierce serpents kill Laocoön and <his> sons.

ante + accusative – before
Lāocoōn, Lāocoontis, m. – Laocoön, a Trojan priest
ligneus, lignea, ligneum – wooden
Minerva, Minervae, f. – Minerva (Athena)
mittō, mittere, mīsī, missum – to send
moneō, monēre, monuī, monitum – to warn
occīdō, occīdere, occīdī, occīsum – to kill

ōdit – s/he hates
porta, portae, f. – gate
positus, posita, positum – positioned, placed
serpēns, serpentis, f. – serpent
Trōia, Trōiae, f. – Troy
Trōiānus, Trōiāna, Trōiānum – Trojan
Trōiānus, Trōiānī, m. – Trojan

▶ EXERCISE 6

Translate into Latin.

1. The fortunate are able to flee. — Fēlīcēs fugere possunt.
2. I do not believe that the Trojans are fortunate. — Trōiānōs esse fēlīcēs nōn crēdō.
   Trōiānus, Trōiānī, m.
3. Flames are destroying Troy. — Flammae Trōiam dēlent.
   Trōia, Trōiae, f.
4. War is not feared by the Trojans. — Bellum ā Trōiānīs nōn timētur.
5. The danger is not understood by the Trojans. — Perīculum ā Trōiānīs nōn intellegitur.
6. Many want to flee. — Multī fugere cupiunt.
7. Not a few Trojans are captured by the enemies. — Nōn paucī Trōiānī ā hostibus capiuntur.

CONTENT QUESTIONS

After completing Chapter 10, answer these questions.

1. Which present forms of *-iō* verbs of the third conjugation resemble the fourth conjugation?
   First person singular and third person plural of the active and passive voice.

2. Where does the main difference between third declension adjectives of one, two and three endings appear?
   In the nominative singular.

3. What group of third declension nouns do the third declension adjectives resemble?
   The *i*-stem nouns, except for the fact that the *-ī* also appears in the ablative singular of the masculine and feminine forms of the adjectives.

4. What famous epic poem deals with the mythical origins of Rome?
   The *Aeneid*.

5. From what eastern race did the Romans believe they had descended?
   From the Trojans, blended with the local inhabitants.

6. Which Greek devised the plan of the wooden horse that brought about the fall of Troy?
   Ulysses. Odysseus is his Greek name.

Ruins of the walls of the ancient city of Troy.

CHAPTER 11

▶ EXERCISE 1

Conjugate the following verbs in the imperfect active and passive voice. Write an English translation for each form.

1. *firmō, firmāre, firmāvī, firmātum*

Imperfect Active: *firmō*

	Singular		Plural	
First person	firmābam	I was strengthening	firmābāmus	we were strengthening
Second person	firmābās	you were strengthening	firmābātis	you were strengthening
Third person	firmābat	s/he/it was strengthening	firmābant	they were strengthening

Imperfect Passive: *firmō*

	Singular		Plural	
First person	firmābar	I was being strengthened	firmābāmur	we were being strengthened
Second person	firmābāris	you were being strengthened	firmābāminī	you were being strengthened
Third person	firmābātur	s/he/it was being strengthened	firmābantur	they were being strengthened

2. *mittō, mittere, mīsī, missum*

Imperfect Active: *mittō*

	Singular		Plural	
First person	mittēbam	I was sending	mittēbāmus	we were sending
Second person	mittēbās	you were sending	mittēbātis	you were sending
Third person	mittēbat	s/he/it was sending	mittēbant	they were sending

Imperfect Passive: *mittō*

	Singular		Plural	
First person	mittēbar	I was being sent	mittēbāmur	we were being sent
Second person	mittēbāris	you were being sent	mittēbāminī	you were being sent
Third person	mittēbātur	s/he/it was being sent	mittēbantur	they were being sent

▶ EXERCISE 2
Translate into English.

1. Timēbāris. — You were being/used to be/kept on being feared.
2. Movēbāminī. — You (pl.) were being/used to be/kept on being moved.
3. Multa sentiēbant. — They were feeling/used to feel/kept on feeling many things.
4. Manēbāmus iacēbāmusque. — We were remaining and lying down.
5. Audīrī quoque poterāmus. — We were also able to be heard.
6. Praeclāra fortisque vidēbātur. — She seemed a distinguished and brave woman.
7. Crūdēlēs nōn erant. — They were not cruel.
8. Relinquēbārisne . . . ? — Were you being left behind . . . ?
9. Nōn erant miserī sed fēlīcēs. — The men were not wretched, but fortunate.
10. Manēre ūnā poterātis. — You were able to remain together.

▶ EXERCISE 3
Translate into Latin.

1. I was conquering. — Vincēbam.
2. It was being told. — Nārrābātur.
3. You (plural) were able to be freed. — Līberārī poterātis.
4. You were being seen. — Vidēbāris.
5. They were burning. — Ardēbant.
6. They were brave. — Fortēs erant.
7. You were able to come. — Venīre poterās.
8. You (plural) were accustomed to know. — Scīre solēbātis.
9. You (plural) were being called. — Vocābāminī.
10. We were being called. — Vocābāmur.

▶ EXERCISE 4
Fill in the blanks using the verb in parentheses and translate each sentence. The Reading Vocabulary may be consulted for names.

Example: Dīdō sē esse rēgīnam fēlīcem __putābat__ (*was thinking*).
Dido was thinking that she was a fortunate queen.

1. Amor Dīdōnis et Aenēae __erat__ māgnus. (*was*)
   The love of Aeneas and Dido was great.

2. Aenēās et Dīdō ad spēluncam __ambulābant__. (*were walking*)
   Aeneas and Dido were walking towards the cave.

3. Aenēās et Dīdō in silvā __erant__. (*were*)
   Aeneas and Dido were in the forest.

4. Tempestās ab Aeneā Dīdōneque __nōn cōnspiciēbātur__. (*was not being observed*)
   The storm was not being observed by Aeneas and Dido.

5. Cīvēs Aenēam cupere terram novam petere __nōn crēdēbant__. (*did not believe*)
   The citizens did not believe that Aeneas desired to seek a new land.

6. Aenēās contrā deōs pugnāre __nōn poterat__. (*was not able*)
   Aeneas was not able to fight against the gods.

Dido and Aeneas as depicted on a seventeenth-century tapestry.

▶ EXERCISE 5

Translate the following passage into Latin.

Aeneas and Dido were wanting to stay together. They seemed to be fortunate to the citizens. Aeneas was not thinking about the words of the gods. The king of the gods understood that Aeneas could not remain with Dido. Dido was unable to overcome the gods, but she grieved greatly. Dido's spirit could not be strengthened. Death seemed to be good to Dido.

Aenēās et Dīdō ūnā manēre cupiēbant. Fēlīcēs esse cīvibus vidēbantur. Aenēās dē deōrum verbīs nōn cōgitābat.

Rēx deōrum intellegēbat Aenēam cum Dīdōne manēre nōn posse. Deōs vincere nōn poterat Dīdō, sed valdē

dolēbat. Animus Dīdōnis firmārī nōn poterat. Mors Dīdōnī bona esse vidēbātur.

Aenēās (acc. Aenēam), m. – Aeneas
Dīdō, Dīdōnis, f. – Dido

Dido on a wall painting from Pompeii.

▶ EXERCISE 6

Choose the best answer for the following questions and translate. The Latin reading passage should be consulted for an accurate response.

1. Eratne Dīdō rēgīna?

    Dīdō rēgīna amōre ārdēbat.

    Dīdō erat rēgīna.

    Dīdō Aenēam valdē amābat.

    Dīdō erat rēgīna.

    Dido was a/the queen.

2. Veniēbatne tempestās māgna?

    Tempestās cōnspiciēbātur.

    Aenēās et Dīdō tempestātem timēbant.

    Tempestās māgna veniēbat.

    Tempestās māgna veniēbat.

    A big storm was coming.

3. Cūr (why) Aenēās et Dīdō in spēluncā manēbant?

    Aenēās et Dīdō in silvā erant.

    Aenēās et Dīdō in silvā ambulābant.

    Aenēās et Dīdō in tempestāte esse nōn cupiēbant.

    Aenēās et Dīdō in tempestāte esse nōn cupiēbant.

    Aeneas and Dido did not want to be in the storm.

50 • Latin for the New Millennium

4. Intellegēbatne Aenēās sē ā Dīdōne amārī?

    Aenēās amōrem Dīdōnis vidēbat.

    Aenēās Dīdōnem amābat.

    Aenēās sē Dīdōnem amāre dīcēbat.

    Aenēās amōrem Dīdōnis vidēbat.

    Aeneas perceived/saw the love of Dido.

5. Cūr (*why*) Aenēās Dīdōque erant fēlīcēs?

    Aenēās et Dīdō saepe ūnā cōnspiciēbantur.

    Aenēās dē deōrum verbīs nōn cōgitābat.

    Aenēās Dīdōque propter amōrem gaudium sentiēbant.

    Aenēās Dīdōque propter amōrem gaudium sentiēbant.

    Aeneas and Dido felt joy because of love.

6. Cūr (*why*) Aenēās Dīdōnem relinquere dēbēbat?

    Aenēās urbem Dīdōnis timēbat.

    Aenēās dē Mercuriī verbīs cōgitābat.

    Aenēās dē terrā novā cōgitābat.

    Aenēās dē Mercuriī verbīs cōgitābat.

    Aeneas was thinking about Mercury's words.

CONTENT QUESTIONS

After completing Chapter 11, answer these questions.

1. In what city was Aeneas welcomed at the court of Dido?
   Carthage.

2. What syllable is the sign of the imperfect tense in all of the conjugations?
   The syllable *-bā-*.

3. What is the meaning of the imperfect tense?
   The imperfect is used for a narrative in the past and represents a continued action.

4. What other verb do the endings of the imperfect tense of *possum* resemble?
   The endings of the imperfect of *possum* look like the imperfect of *sum*.

5. What is an enclitic?
   An enclitic is a particle that is attached to the preceding word.

6. What do the enclitics *-que* and *-ne* mean?
   The enclitic *–que* means "and"; the enclitic *–ne* attached to the first word of a sentence makes

   the sentence a question.

CHAPTER 12

▶ EXERCISE 1

Decline the following phrases.

1. *nōmen meum*

	Singular	Plural
Nominative	nōmen meum	nōmina mea
Genitive	nōminis meī	nōminum meōrum
Dative	nōminī meō	nōminibus meīs
Accusative	nōmen meum	nōmina mea
Ablative	nōmine meō	nōminibus meīs

2. *ignis tuus*

	Singular	Plural
Nominative	ignis tuus	ignēs tuī
Genitive	ignis tuī	ignium tuōrum
Dative	ignī tuō	ignibus tuīs
Accusative	ignem tuum	ignēs tuōs
Ablative	igne tuō	ignibus tuīs

3. *īra nostra*

	Singular	Plural
Nominative	īra nostra	īrae nostrae
Genitive	īrae nostrae	īrārum nostrārum
Dative	īrae nostrae	īrīs nostrīs
Accusative	īram nostram	īrās nostrās
Ablative	īrā nostrā	īrīs nostrīs

4. *vīs vestra*

	Singular	Plural
Nominative	vīs vestra	vīrēs vestrae
Genitive	—	vīrium vestrārum
Dative	—	vīribus vestrīs
Accusative	vim vestram	vīrēs vestrās
Ablative	vī vestrā	vīribus vestrīs

▶ EXERCISE 2
Translate into English.

1. Casa ab eō aedificātur. — The dwelling is being built by him.
2. Rēx meās fīliās nōn videt. — The king does not see my daughters.
3. Mulier tibi similis est. — The woman is like you.
4. Fortitūdine tuā docēmur. — We are taught by your bravery.
5. Flammārum vim nōn timeō. — I do not fear the force of the flames.
6. Vōs nōn timeō. — I do not fear you (pl.).
7. Animum meum prō vīribus firmō. — I am strengthening my spirit with all my might.

▶ EXERCISE 3
Translate into Latin.

1. to/for my pain — dolōrī meō
2. of your word — verbī tuī
3. your (plural) friends — amīcī vestrī
4. by/with my sister — sorōre meā
5. of your (plural) gifts — dōnōrum vestrōrum
6. It was being observed by our son. — Id ā fīliō nostrō cōnspiciēbātur.
7. I think about your prize. — Dē praemiō tuō cōgitō.
8. My daughters are loved by me. — Meae fīliae ā mē amantur.

▶ EXERCISE 4
Supply the correct corresponding form of *is, ea, id* in the following phrases.

1. those things — ea
2. by/with that woman — eā
3. of those people — eōrum
4. of those women — eārum
5. of those things — eōrum
6. by/with these people — eīs (iīs)
7. his — ēius
8. hers — ēius
9. to him — eī
10. to her — eī
11. to it — eī
12. she — ea
13. by/with this man — eō
14. by/with that thing — eō

Mucius Scaevola places his hand in the fire in front
of the king of the Etruscans.

▶ EXERCISE 5

Translate the following passage into English.

Mūcius erat cīvis Rōmānus et homō fortis. In Etrūscōrum castra intrat. Rēgem Etrūscōrum occīdere cupit, nec ēius mīlitēs timet. Sed hostium vīrēs nōn intellegit. Itaque Mūcius ab hostibus capitur. Rēx Etrūscōrum Mūcium ad sē vocat. "Tū es mihi hostis," inquit, "et hostium meōrum nōmina mihi dīcere dēbēs." Ignēs prope Mūcium ā mīlitibus Etrūscīs pōnuntur. Mūcius autem nec ignēs nec rēgis īram timet. "Vī," inquit Mūcius, "mē vincere nōn potes."

Mucius was a Roman citizen and a brave man. He goes into the camp of the Etruscans. He wants to kill the king of the Etruscans, nor does he fear his soldiers. But he does not realize the strength of the enemies. And so Mucius is captured by the enemies. The king of the Etruscans summons Mucius to him. "You are an enemy to me," he says, "and you must tell me the names of my enemies." Fires are positioned near Mucius by the Etruscan soldiers. But Mucius fears neither the fires nor the king's anger. "You cannot overcome me by violence," says Mucius.

nec . . . nec . . . – neither . . . nor . . .

▶ EXERCISE 6

Choose the best answer for the following questions and translate. The Latin reading passage in Chapter 12 should be consulted for an accurate response.

1. Rēgemne Etrūscōrum timēbat Mūcius?

    Etrūscī semper timēbant.

    Rōmānī hostēs timēbant.

    Mūcius rēgem nōn timēbat.

    Mūcius rēgem nōn timēbat.

    Mucius was not afraid of the king.

2. Cupiēbatne Mūcius rēgem Etrūscōrum servāre?

    Mūcius fortitūdinem ostendere cupiēbat.

    Mūcius rēgem hostium occīdere cupiēbat.

    Mūcius in Etrūscōrum castra intrāre cupiēbat.

    Mūcius rēgem hostium occīdere cupiēbat.

    Mucius wanted to kill the king of the enemies.

3. Suntne Rōmānī Mūciō similēs?

    Rōmānī sunt multī Mūciō similēs.

    Rōmānī rēgem Etrūscōrum timent.

    Rōmānī sunt Etrūscīs similēs.

    Rōmānī sunt multī Mūciō similēs.

    There are many Romans like Mucius.

4. Dēbēbatne rēx Etrūscōrum cīvēs Rōmānōs semper timēre?

    Rēx Etrūscōrum cīvēs Rōmānōs semper timēre nōn dēbēbat.

    Rēx Etrūscōrum hostēs semper timēre dēbēbat.

    Rēx Etrūscōrum īrā semper movētur.

    Rēx Etrūscōrum hostēs semper timēre dēbēbat.

    The king of the Etruscans always had to fear enemies.

5. Dēbēbatne rēx Etrūscōrum hostēs domī timēre?

    Rēx Etrūscōrum hostēs occīdere cupiēbat.

    Rēx Etrūscōrum perīculum timēre nōn dēbēbat.

    Rēx Etrūscōrum hostēs in castrīs et domī timēre dēbēbat.

    Rēx Etrūscōrum hostēs in castrīs et domī timēre dēbēbat.

    The king of the Etruscans had to fear enemies in the camp and at home.

6. Dīcitne rēx Etrūscōrum Mūciō ex ignibus esse perīculum?

    Rēx Etrūscōrum flammās semper timēbat.

    Rēx Etrūscōrum dīcit Mūcium ignēs timēre dēbēre.

    Dīcit rēx Etrūscōrum Mūcium ē castrīs fugere dēbēre.

    Rēx Etrūscōrum dīcit Mūcium ignēs timēre dēbēre.

    The king of the Etruscans says that Mucius should fear the fires.

7. Crēdēbatne rēx Mūciī fortitūdinem vincī posse?

    Crēdēbat rēx sē hostēs fortēs vincere posse.

    Intellegit rēx sē Mūcium vincere nōn posse.

    Rēx Rōmānōs nōn esse fortēs putat.

    Intellegit rēx sē Mūcium vincere nōn posse.

    The king understands that he cannot conquer Mucius.

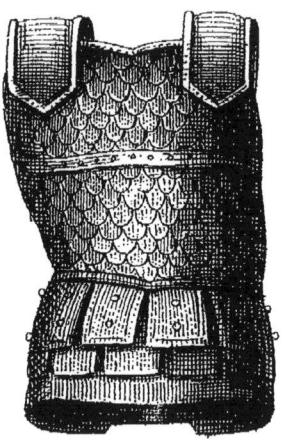

Etruscan soldier's breastplate.

CONTENT QUESTIONS

After completing Chapter 12, answer these questions.

1. Why is the noun *vīs* called defective?
   It is lacking several of its forms.

2. The demonstrative *is, ea, id* has forms that you have already seen in declensions of nouns. In which declensions can we find forms parallel to those of *is, ea, id*?
   In the first, second, and third declensions.

3. What case endings of *is, ea, id* are not paralleled in any of the declensions you have seen so far?
   The genitive and dative singular endings.

4. What did the Roman historian Livy apparently believe about the Roman morals of his own day?
   He thought they were very inferior to the simple virtues of the early Romans.

5. With which Roman emperor did Livy have connections?
   The emperor Augustus.

6. What was the title of Livy's work, and what does it mean?
   Ab urbe conditā, "From the Founding of the City."

Rome was founded in 753 BCE. In the Roman calendar, years were calculated from this starting point: A.U.C., Ab urbe conditā, i.e., from 753 BCE. For example, the year 700 A.U.C. would be 53 BCE.

CHAPTER 13

▶ EXERCISE 1

Give the positive and negative imperatives of the following verbs.

		Positive Imperative		Negative Imperative	
		Singular	Plural	Singular	Plural
1.	intrō, intrāre, intrāvī, intrātum	intrā	intrāte	nōlī intrāre	nōlīte intrāre
2.	doceō, docēre, docuī, doctum	docē	docēte	nōlī docēre	nōlīte docēre
3.	mittō, mittere, mīsī, missum	mitte	mittite	nōlī mittere	nōlīte mittere
4.	fugiō, fugere, fūgī, ——	fuge	fugite	nōlī fugere	nōlīte fugere
5.	veniō, venīre, vēnī, ventum	venī	venīte	nōlī venīre	nōlīte venīre

▶ EXERCISE 2

Change the positive or negative singular imperatives into the plural and the plural forms into the singular. Translate the changed forms.

Example: nāvigāte!
nāvigā!   sail!

1. vidē! — vidēte!   see (pl.)!
2. mitte! — mittite!   send (pl.)!
3. ostende! — ostendite!   show (pl.)!
4. habitāte! — habitā!   inhabit!
5. audī! — audīte!   hear (pl.)!
6. nōlī iubēre! — nōlīte iubēre!   do not order (pl.)!
7. cōnspice! — cōnspicite!   observe (pl.)!
8. dēlē! — dēlēte!   destroy (pl.)!
9. cupite! — cupe!   desire!
10. nōlīte dolēre! — nōlī dolēre!   do not feel pain!
11. nārrā! — nārrāte!   tell (pl.)!

> Some of the sentences on the next page (Exercise 4) are adapted from Horace, *Ode* 3.30.
>> Exēgī monumentum aere perennius ...
>> "I have made <myself> a monument more lasting than bronze ..."
> aes, aeris, n. – bronze
> exēgī – perfect active indicative, first person singular of *exigō, exigere, exēgī, exāctum*, "to bring to an end, to make"
> perennius – accusative neuter singular, comparative degree of *perennis, perenne*, "lasting"; the second term of comparison is in the ablative
>> Nōn omnis moriar ...
>> "I will not die all ..."
> moriar – future active indicative, first person singular of *morior, morī, mortuus sum*, "to die"

▶ EXERCISE 3

Fill in the blanks with either a form of *suus, sua, suum* or with *ēius, eōrum, eārum* and translate the sentences.

Example: Vir dē cōnsiliō ___suō___ cōgitat.
The man thinks of/about his plan.

1. Rōmānī contrā hostēs pugnant et ___eōrum___ urbem dēlent.
   The Romans fight against the enemies and destroy their city.

2. Dīvitēs praemia ___sua___ servāre cupiunt.
   Rich people desire to save their rewards.

3. Agricola terram ___suam___ cūrat, āthlēta corpus suum.
   The farmer is taking care of his land, the athlete of his body.

4. Poēta virum audiēbat et ___ēius___ verba nōn amābat.
   The poet was listening to the man and did not like his words.

5. Doctī librōs ___suōs___ semper tenent.
   Learned people always keep their books.

6. Ducēs mīlitēs ___suōs___ dūcunt.
   The leaders lead their soldiers.

▶ EXERCISE 4

Translate into Latin. (Some are Horace's own thoughts.)

1. The poet builds his monument.
   monumentum, monumentī, n. – monument

   Poēta monumentum suum aedificat.

2. The poet builds a monument and the monument can remain forever.

   Poēta monumentum aedificat et monumentum semper manēre potest.

3. Not all parts of me have to die.
   pars, partis, f. – part   morī – to die

   Nōn omnēs partēs meī dēbent morī.

4. Not all parts of us must die.

   Nōn omnēs partēs nostrum dēbent morī.

5. Who of you (plural) does not desire to live always?
   quis? – who?

   Quis vestrum nōn cupit semper vīvere?

6. I say these words because of love for/of you.

   Ea verba propter amōrem tuī dīcō.

A Roman shield such as the one that Horace says he threw down in battle.

▶ EXERCICE 5

Translate into English the following anecdote related to an event in Horace's life.

Horātius erat mīlēs et in bellō pugnāre dēbēbat. Is tamen cōgitābat: "Multī nostrum in bellō occīduntur. Ducēs nōs pugnāre iubent, sed verba eōrum audīre nōn dēbēmus. Ūnusquisque nostrum corpus suum servāre potest. Bonum et pulchrum est prō patriā morī, sed propter amōrem meī vītam meam habēre cupiō." Tunc poēta scūtum suum relinquit et fugit.

Horace was a soldier and had to fight in a war. However, he thought: "Many of us are being killed in the war. The commanders order us to fight, but we should not listen to their words. Each one of us can save his body. It is good and noble to die for the fatherland, but because of love for myself I want to have my life." Then the poet leaves his shield behind and flees.

Horātius, Horātiī, m. – Horace
morī – to die

scūtum, scūtī, n. – shield
ūnusquisque – each one

The material of this text is derived from *Ode* 2.7 and *Ode* 3.2.

Horace wrote in *Satire* I.9 that he was walking along the *Via Sacra* in the Roman Forum. The *Via Sacra* runs on a slight diagonal in this picture—from the grove of trees in the upper right corner into the forum at the left.

▶ EXERCISE 6

For each question, choose the best answer and translate. Refer to the Latin reading passage, if necessary.

1. Ubi (*where*) erat Horātius?

    Horātius in sacrō templō erat.

    Horātius in agrīs erat.

    Horātius in viā erat.

    Horātius in spēluncā erat.

    Horātius in viā erat.

    Horace was on the road.

2. Quid cupiēbat importūnus?

    Poētae importūnus verba dīcere cupiēbat.

    Importūnus pugnāre cupiēbat.

    Importūnus ambulāre nōn cupiēbat.

    Importūnus cōnsilia capere cupiēbat.

    Poētae importūnus verba dīcere cupiēbat.

    The boor wanted to say words to the poet.

Teacher's Manual • Chapter 13 • 61

3. Quid cupiēbat Horātius?

    Horātius verba dīcere cupiēbat.

    Horātius nihil cūrābat.

    Horātius fugere cupiēbat.

    Horātius ōrātiōnem habēre cupiēbat.

    Horātius fugere cupiēbat.

    Horace desired to flee.

4. Quid Horātius dē Maecēnāte dīcēbat?

    Horātius Maecēnātem nōn amābat.

    Horātius ā Maecēnāte fugere cupiēbat.

    Horātius nihil dē Maecēnāte sciēbat.

    Horātius dē Maecēnātis domō bona verba dīcēbat.

    Horātius dē Maecēnātis domō bona verba dīcēbat.

    Horace was saying good words about the house of Maecenas.

5. Quōmodo (*how*) Horātius servātur?

    Alius homō importūnum ad iūdicem vocat.

    Importūnus ad casam fugit.

    Iūdex importūnum līberat.

    Horātius importūnum discēdere iubet.

    Alius homō importūnum ad iūdicem vocat.

    Another man calls the boor to the judge.

CONTENT QUESTIONS

After completing Chapter 13, answer these questions.

1. What does the grammatical term "mood" mean?

   The mood indicates whether the action expressed by the verb is represented as really happening, or as desired to happen.

2. Which moods of the verb do you know by now?

   Indicative and imperative.

3. What words are used to form the negative imperative?

   Nōlī, nōlīte.

4. Who was Maecenas?

   Maecenas was a rich man who sponsored poets during the time of Augustus.

5. What was Horace's ideal in life?

   Equilibrium or balance and moderation, *aurea mediocritās*, "golden mean."

6. What characterizes the literature of Augustan times?

   It is focused on individual human concerns and emotions.

CHAPTER 14

▶ EXERCISE 1

Conjugate the following verbs in the future active and passive, singular and plural. Write an English translation for each form.

1. *līberō, līberāre, līberāvī, līberātum*

Future Active: *līberō*

	Singular		Plural	
First person	līberābō	I will/shall free	līberābimus	we will/shall free
Second person	līberābis	you will free	līberābitis	you will free
Third person	līberābit	s/he/it will free	līberābunt	they will free

Future Passive: *līberō*

	Singular		Plural	
First person	līberābor	I will/shall be freed	līberābimur	we will/shall be freed
Second person	līberāberis	you will be freed	līberābiminī	you will be freed
Third person	līberābitur	s/he/it will be freed	līberābuntur	they will be freed

2. *iubeō, iubēre, iussī, iussum*

Future Active: *iubeō*

	Singular		Plural	
First person	iubēbō	I will/shall order	iubēbimus	we will/shall order
Second person	iubēbis	you will order	iubēbitis	you will order
Third person	iubēbit	s/he/it will order	iubēbunt	they will order

Future Passive: *iubeō*

	Singular		Plural	
First person	iubēbor	I will/shall be ordered	iubēbimur	we will/shall be ordered
Second person	iubēberis	you will be ordered	iubēbiminī	you will be ordered
Third person	iubēbitur	s/he/it will be ordered	iubēbuntur	they will be ordered

▶ EXERCISE 2

Identify the case, number, and gender of the following forms of the relative pronoun. Give all possible answers.

Example: quae
feminine singular nominative   feminine plural nominative   neuter plural nominative
neuter plural accusative

1. quō — masculine singular ablative; neuter singular ablative
2. quī — masculine singular nominative; masculine plural nominative
3. cūius — masculine singular genitive; feminine singular genitive; neuter singular genitive
4. quā — feminine singular ablative
5. cui — masculine singular dative; feminine singular dative; neuter singular dative
6. quōrum — masculine plural genitive; neuter plural genitive
7. quibus — masculine plural dative and ablative; feminine plural dative and ablative; neuter plural dative and ablative
8. quod — neuter singular nominative; neuter singular accusative
9. quam — feminine singular accusative
10. quem — masculine singular accusative

▶ EXERCISE 3

Change the singular forms into plural and the plural into singular. Translate the changed form.

Example: ārdēbis
ārdēbitis   you (plural) will burn

1. cōgitābit — cōgitābunt: they will think
2. firmābiminī — firmāberis: you will be strengthened
3. iūdicābis — iūdicābitis: you (pl.) will judge
4. dolēbimus — dolēbō: I will/shall feel pain
5. docēbunt — docēbit: s/he/it will teach
6. manēbō — manēbimus: we will/shall remain
7. poteris — poteritis: you (pl.) will be able
8. poterunt — poterit: s/he/it will be able
9. erit — erunt: they will be
10. līberāberis — līberābiminī: you (pl.) will be freed
11. rogābitur — rogābuntur: they will be asked

▶ EXERCISE 4

Change the forms in the active voice into passive and the passive forms into the active voice. Translate the changed form.

Example: habēbiminī
habēbitis   you (plural) will have

1. dēlēbuntur — dēlēbunt: they will delete
2. dabit — dabitur (The students should be reminded that *dō* has a short *a* in its stem): s/he/it will be given
3. vocābimus — vocābimur: we will/shall be called
4. docēbis — docēberis: you will be taught
5. iubēbiminī — iubēbitis: you (pl.) will order
6. putābō — putābor: I will/shall be considered
7. servābunt — servābuntur: they will be saved
8. sēparāberis — sēparābis: you will separate
9. docēbor — docēbō: I will/shall teach
10. nārrābimur — nārrābimus: we will/shall tell
11. amābitur — amābit: s/he/it will love

▶ EXERCISE 5

Choose which one of the four statements is true based on the Latin reading passage and translate the statement. The Reading Vocabulary may be consulted.

1. Parentēs Pȳramī Thisbēn amant.

   Parentēs Thisbēs Pȳramum amant.

   Puer ā puellā, quam amat, pariete sēparātur.

   Inter Pȳramum et Thisbēn est odium.

   Puer ā puellā, quam amat, pariete sēparātur.
   The boy is separated from the girl he loves by a wall.

2. Pȳramus Thisbēn tenēbit.

   Pȳramus Thisbēn nōn vidēbit.

   Pȳramus leaenam vidēbit.

   Pȳramus erit in spēluncā.

   Pȳramus Thisbēn nōn vidēbit.
   Pyramus will not see Thisbe.

3. Pӯramus et Thisbē convenīre dēbent prope arborem, in quā sunt pōma rubra.

   In arbore sunt pōma alba et pōma rubra.

   Pōma, quae erant alba, mox erunt rubra.

   Pōma, quae erant rubra, mox erunt alba.

   Pōma, quae erant alba, mox erunt rubra.

   The berries which were white will soon be red.

4. Pӯramus, quī leaenam timet, fugit.

   Pӯramus et Thisbe ā leaenā fugiunt.

   Thisbē leaenam nōn videt.

   Thisbē, quae leaenam videt, fugit.

   Thisbē, quae leaenam videt, fugit.

   Thisbe, who sees the lioness, flees.

5. Pӯramus iam nōn cupit vīvere.

   Leaena Pӯramum comedit.

   Leaena Thisbēn comedit.

   Pӯramus leaenam occīdit.

   Pӯramus iam nōn cupit vīvere.

   Pӯramus does not want to live now.

6. Thisbē sē occīdit.

   Leaena Thisbēn comedit.

   Thisbē Pӯramum gladiō occīdit.

   Thisbē Pӯramō gladium dat.

   Thisbē sē occīdit.

   Thisbe kills herself.

Thisbe stands next to the wall that separates her from Pyramus.

▶ EXERCISE 6

Fill in the blanks with the correct case, number, and gender of the relative pronoun and translate the sentences. The Reading Vocabulary may be consulted.

Example: Thisbē, ____quae____ prope Pȳramum habitābat, ab eō amābātur.
Thisbe, who lived close to Pyramus, was beloved by him.

1. Pȳramus et Thisbē nōn amābant parietem, ____quō____ sēparābantur.
   Pyramus and Thisbe did not love the wall, by which they were separated.

2. Pariēs, ____cui____ Pȳramus et Thisbē verba dīcēbant, nōn respondēbat.
   The wall, to which Pyramus and Thisbe were saying words, did not answer.

3. Leaena appropinquābit ad puellam, ____quae____ exspectābit.
   A lioness will approach the girl, who will be waiting.

4. Vēlāmen, ____quod____ puella habēbat, in terram cadit.
   The veil, which the girl had, falls onto the ground.

5. Thisbē sē occīdit gladiō, ____quō____ Pȳramus sē occīdit.
   Thisbe kills herself with the sword, with which Pyramus kills himself.

A profile of Publius Ovidius Nāso, author of the *Metamorphōsēs*.

CONTENT QUESTIONS

After completing Chapter 14, answer these questions.

1. What does the title *Metamorphōsēs* mean, whose work is it, and why is it called by this name?

    "Transformations." A poetic work on mythology by Ovid. Describes transformations of heroes or heroines into animals, plants, stars, etc.

2. Name an important event in Ovid's life.

    Ovid was sent into exile to the Black Sea, where he wrote many poems full of sorrowful reflections and complaints.

3. How do you form the future indicative of the first and the second conjugation?

    You add to the stem -bō, -bis, -bit, -bimus, -bitis, -bunt for the active voice, and -bor, -beris, -bitur, -bimur, -biminī, -buntur for the passive voice.

4. Which noun declensions do the forms of the relative pronoun resemble?

    First, second, and third; some forms of the relative pronoun's declension, however, do not resemble any of these declensions.

5. What is an antecedent?

    An antecedent is a word in the main clause to which the relative pronoun in the relative clause refers.

6. What determines the case, number, and gender of the relative pronoun?

    The relative pronoun has the same number and gender as the antecedent. Its case depends on its function in the relative clause.

CHAPTER 15

▶ EXERCISE 1

Conjugate the following verbs in the future active and passive, singular and plural. Write an English translation for each form.

1. *relinquō, relinquere, relīquī, relictum*

Future Active: *relinquō*

	Singular			Plural	
First person	relinquam	I will/shall leave	relinquēmus	we will/shall leave
Second person	relinquēs	you will leave	relinquētis	you will leave
Third person	relinquet	s/he/it will leave	relinquent	they will leave

Future Passive: *relinquō*

	Singular			Plural	
First person	relinquar	I will/shall be left	relinquēmur	we will/shall be left
Second person	relinquēris	you will be left	relinquēminī	you will be left
Third person	relinquētur	s/he/it will be left	relinquentur	they will be left

2. *sciō, scīre, scīvī, scītum*

Future Active: *sciō*

	Singular			Plural	
First person	sciam	I will/shall know	sciēmus	we will/shall know
Second person	sciēs	you will know	sciētis	you will know
Third person	sciet	s/he/it will know	scient	they will know

Future Passive: *sciō*

	Singular			Plural	
First person	sciar	I will/shall be known	sciēmur	we will/shall be known
Second person	sciēris	you will be known	sciēminī	you will be known
Third person	sciētur	s/he/it will be known	scientur	they will be known

▶ EXERCISE 2
Translate into Latin.

1. Whose country house is neglected?
   Cūius vīlla neglegitur?

2. What country house is neglected?
   Quae vīlla neglegitur?

3. Which country houses are neglected?
   Quae vīllae negleguntur?

4. Whose (plural) country houses are neglected?
   Quōrum vīllae negleguntur?

5. To whom is the country house being given?
   Cui vīlla datur?

6. To whom (plural) are the country houses being given?
   Quibus vīllae dantur?

7. By what man is the country house being given to me?
   Ā quō vīlla mihi datur?

8. By what woman is the country house being given to me?
   Ā quā vīlla mihi datur?

9. By which people is the country house being given to me?
   Ā quibus vīlla mihi datur?

10. What country house do we see?
    Quam vīllam vidēmus?

11. Which country houses do we see?
    Quās vīllās vidēmus?

12. From which country houses are they coming?
    Ē quibus vīllīs veniunt?

13. Who is living in the country house?
    Quis in vīllā habitat?

14. Who are living in the country house?
    Quī in vīllā habitant?

15. With what man were you fleeing?
    Quōcum virō fugiēbās?

16. With what woman will you flee?
    Quācum muliere fugiēs?

► EXERCISE 3

Change the verbs in the imperfect tense into the future, keeping the same person, number, and voice. Translate the changed forms.

Example: ostendēbantur
ostendentur   they will be shown

1. cōnspiciēbāminī — cōnspiciēminī: you (pl.) will be observed
2. fugiēbant — fugient: they will flee
3. pōnēbātis — pōnētis: you will place
4. capiēbāmur — capiēmur: we will/shall be taken
5. mittēbāris — mittēris: you will be sent
6. vincēbāmur — vincēmur: we will/shall be conquered
7. neglegēbat — negleget: s/he will neglect
8. petēbāris — petēris: you will be sought
9. tangēbam — tangam: I will/shall touch

► EXERCISE 4

Translate into Latin.

1. An indication of old age.
   Senectūtis argūmentum.
2. The stones of my villa.
   Saxa vīllae meae.
3. The small country houses.
   Vīllae parvae.
4. Which rural roads?
   Quae viae rūsticae?
5. About the trees which we see.
   Dē arboribus quās vidēmus.
6. Which (things) are true?
   Quae sunt vēra?
7. Look here! The country house of Seneca!
   Ecce vīlla Senecae!
8. Do not, friends, look at the old man who is standing by the country house.
   Nōlīte, amīcī, senem cōnspicere, quī prope vīllam stat.

Seneca, first the tutor and later the advisor to the emperor Nero, was accused of conspiracy and was asked to slit his wrists. When he did not die quickly enough, he is said to have settled into a tub of warm water in order to make the blood flow faster.

▶ EXERCISE 5

Translate the following passage into Latin. Use the Vocabulary to Learn and the words listed below the passage.

I shall come to my country house, and there will be joy for me. I always said and I always shall say that I love the rural life. However, I always had to live in the city because of official duties. But now there is leisure for me. So I shall flee from the city and I shall seek my rural land. I shall leave the civic life. I shall remain in my country house and I shall live there. What will I do there? What friends will I have? The farmers will be <my> friends, with whom I shall take care of the trees. There will be fields there, which I shall observe with joy.

Veniam in vīllam meam et ibi mihi erit gaudium. Semper dīcēbam semperque dīcam mē vītam rūsticam amāre.

In urbe autem propter officia cīvīlia semper habitāre dēbēbam. Sed nunc mihi est ōtium. Itaque ex urbe fugiam

terramque meam rūsticam petam. Vītam cīvīlem relinquam. In vīllā meā manēbō et habitābō. Quid ibi faciam?

Quōs amīcōs habēbō? Agricolae erunt amīcī, quibuscum arborēs cūrābō. Agrī ibi erunt, quōs cum gaudiō cōnspiciam.

cīvīlis, cīvīle – civic, official, public
officium, officiī, n. – duty

ōtium, ōtiī, n. – leisure

The teacher may mention *ex officiō*, "by the right of office."

The Villa of Diomedes lies outside Pompeii on the south side of the Roman road, today called the Via dei Sepolcri, that led to Herculaneum. The villa sits beyond the last group of tombs on the left of the road and opposite the tomb of Marcus Arrius Diomedes, for whom the villa is named. The large villa is known for its fresco series and for its grand size and scale including a set of private baths.

▶ EXERCISE 6

Choose which one of the three statements is true based on the Latin Reading passage and translate the statement. The Reading Vocabulary may be consulted.

1. Senectūtem timēre dēbēmus.

    Contrā senectūtem pugnāre nōn dēbēmus.

    Vīlla ā Senecā neglegitur.

    Contrā senectūtem pugnāre nōn dēbēmus.

    We should not fight against old age.

2. Senex, quī ante Senecam stat, senectūtem nōn amat.

    Difficile Senecae est senem, quī prope vīllam stat, vidēre.

    Seneca cum homine, quī prope vīllam stat, quondam ludēbat puer.

    Seneca cum homine, quī prope vīllam stat, quondam ludēbat puer.

    Seneca as a boy once played with the man who is standing near the villa.

3. Senex, quī prope vīllam stat, Senecam spectat.

    Iānua, prope quam stat senex, ā Senecā nōn cōgnōscitur.

    Arborēs sunt prope iānuam.

    Senex, quī prope vīllam stat, Senecam spectat.

    The old man who is standing near the villa is staring at Seneca.

74 • Latin for the New Millennium

4. Vīlla Senecae vidēbātur dē senectūte dīcere.
   Vīlla Senecae vidēbātur senectūtem exspectāre.
   Vīlla Senecae vidēbātur saxa nōn habēre.

   Vīlla Senecae vidēbātur dē senectūte dīcere.

   Seneca's villa seemed to speak about old age.

5. Seneca dīcit arborēs prope vīllam cadere.
   Seneca dīcit sē arborēs prope vīllam posuisse.
   Vīlicus dīcit sē arborēs prope vīllam posuisse.

   Seneca dīcit sē arborēs prope vīllam posuisse.

   Seneca says that he planted the trees near the villa.

6. Arborēs ā vīlicō nōn cūrābantur.
   Arborēs ā vīlicō nōn semper cūrābantur.
   Arborēs ā vīlicō cūrābantur.

   Arborēs ā vīlicō cūrābantur.

   The trees were cared for by the steward.

The tomb of Lucius Annaeus Seneca,
built alongside the Via Appia.

▶ EXERCISE 7

In the following passage you are going to read about some habits of Roman senators. The passage is written from the point of view of a modern historian, so all the verbs are in the imperfect tense. Rewrite the passage changing all the verbs into the future tense. You can imagine that you are Romulus, the legendary founder of Rome, predicting the future habits of the senators of the state you have founded. Finally, translate the rewritten passage into English.

Senātōrēs Rōmānī nōn paucī nōn sōlum in urbe habitābant, sed etiam vīllās habēbant. In urbe multa faciēbant. Ibi enim officia cīvīlia cūrāre dēbēbant. Multī autem eōrum tumultum et perīcula urbis nōn amābant. Nam terram rūsticam amābant, in quā erat tranquillitās. Itaque vīllās saepe petere cupiēbant. Interdum urbem relinquēbant et diū in vīllīs manēbant, in quibus dē litterīs et dē philosophiā cōgitāre poterant. In terrā rūsticā sē vītam vēram habēre sentiēbant. Terram rūsticam esse patriam vēram crēdēbant.

Senātōrēs Rōmānī nōn paucī nōn sōlum in urbe habitābunt, sed etiam vīllās habēbunt. In urbe multa facient.

Ibi enim officia cīvīlia cūrāre dēbēbunt. Multī autem eōrum tumultum et perīcula urbis nōn amābunt.

Nam terram rūsticam amābunt, in quā erit tranquillitās. Itaque vīllās saepe petere cupient. Interdum urbem

relinquent et diū in vīllīs manēbunt, in quibus dē litterīs et dē philosophiā cōgitāre poterunt. In terrā rūsticā

sē vītam vēram habēre sentient. Terram rūsticam esse patriam vēram crēdent.

Not a few Roman senators shall not only live in the city, but they will also have country houses. They will do many things in the city. For there they will have to take care of political duties. Many of them, however, will not love the disturbance and the dangers of the city. For they will love the rural region, in which there will be tranquillity. Therefore they will often want to go to <their> country houses. Sometimes they shall leave the city behind and will remain for a long time in the country houses, in which they will be able to think about literature and philosophy. In the rural region they will feel they have true life. They shall believe that the rural region is <their> true fatherland.

cīvīlis, cīvīle – civil, political
interdum (adv.) – sometimes
officium, officiī, n. – duty
philosophia, philosophiae, f. – philosophy

senātor, senātōris, m. – senator (derived from *senex*, since the senate was a "council of elders")
tranquillitās, tranquillitātis, f. – peacefulness, tranquillity
tumultus, tumultūs, m. – uproar, disturbance

The teacher may mention that although *tumultus* looks like a second declension noun, it is actually in the fourth declension.

CONTENT QUESTIONS

After completing Chapter 15, answer these questions.

1. In what form did Seneca write his philosophical essays?
   He wrote them in the form of letters.

2. What public role did Seneca play in the time of Nero?
   He was an advisor to the emperor.

3. What are the vowels that appear in the endings of the future of the third and fourth conjugation?
   The vowels are *-a* and *-e*.

4. The future tense forms of the *-iō* verbs of the third conjugation are identical to the future forms of what other conjugation?
   They look like the future tense forms of the fourth conjugation.

5. Why is there no feminine form in the singular of the interrogative pronoun?
   An unspecified question beginning with *quis* is actually asking about a human being in general without reference to gender.

6. To what other form is the interrogative adjective identical?
   It looks just like the relative pronoun.

CHAPTER 16

▶ EXERCISE 1

Conjugate the following verbs in the perfect active and translate each form.

1. *deleō, delēre, delēvī, delētum*

Perfect Active: *dēleō*

Singular

First person	dēlēvī	I destroyed, did destroy, have destroyed
Second person	dēlēvistī	you destroyed, did destroy, have destroyed
Third person	dēlēvit	s/he/it destroyed, did destroy, has destroyed

Plural

First person	dēlēvimus	we destroyed, did destroy, have destroyed
Second person	dēlēvistis	you destroyed, did destroy, have destroyed
Third person	dēlēvērunt	they destroyed, did destroy, have destroyed

2. *discēdō, discēdere, discessī, discessum*

Perfect Active: *discēdō*

Singular

First person	discessī	I left, did leave, have left
Second person	discessistī	you left, did leave, have left
Third person	discessit	s/he/it left, did leave, has left

Plural

First person	discessimus	we left, did leave, have left
Second person	discessistis	you left, did leave, have left
Third person	discessērunt	they left, did leave, has left

3. *veniō, venīre, vēnī, ventum*

Perfect Active: *veniō*

Singular

First person	vēnī	I came, did come, have come
Second person	vēnistī	you came, did come, have come
Third person	vēnit	s/he/it came, did come, has come

Plural

First person	vēnimus	we came, did come, have come
Second person	vēnistis	you came, did come, have come
Third person	vēnērunt	they came, did come, have come

▶ EXERCISE 2
Translate into Latin.

1. They waited for the old man. — Senem exspectāvērunt.
2. He said nothing. — Nihil dīxit.
3. We understood everything (all things). — Omnia intellēximus.
4. You did not send the letter. — Epistulam nōn mīsistī.
5. They saw the sea. — Mare vīdērunt.
6. You (plural) never answered. — Numquam respondistis.
7. You ordered the soldier to speak. — Iussistī mīlitem dīcere.
8. He left the shore. — Lītus relīquit.
9. Stones fell from the mountain. — Saxa ē monte cecidērunt.
10. The conflagration destroyed ships. — Incendium nāvēs dēlēvit.

A square-rigged Roman ship.

▶ EXERCISE 3

Change the imperfect active verbs into the corresponding perfect active, keeping the same person and number. Translate the changed form.

Example: sentiēbātis
sēnsistis   you (plural) felt *or* did feel *or* have felt

1. tangēbat — tetigit — s/he/it touched, did touch, has touched
2. habitābāmus — habitāvimus — we inhabited, did inhabit, have inhabited
3. agēbātis — ēgistis — you (pl.) did, did do, have done
4. dabam — dedī — I gave, did give, have given
5. docēbāmus — docuimus — we taught, did teach, have taught
6. stābam — stetī — I stood, did stand, have stood
7. faciēbant — fēcērunt — they made, did make, have made
8. dēbēbās — dēbuistī — you owed, did owe, have owed / you had to
9. dīcēbās — dīxistī — you said, did say, have said

▶ EXERCISE 4

Fill in the blanks with the correct form of the perfect tense and translate the completed sentence.

Example: Nōs saxa et cinerēs in lītore vidēre __potuimus__. (posse)
We were able (could) to see the stones and ashes on the shore.

1. Clādēs __fuit__ māgna et fūnesta. (esse)
   The disaster was great and deadly.

2. Eō tempore multae nāvēs prope nōs __fuērunt__. Posteā nihil vidēre __potuimus__. (esse, posse)
   At that time many ships were near to us. Afterwards we were able (could) to see nothing.

3. Ego epistulam tuam __lēgī__; tū autem meam numquam __lēgistī__. (legere, legere)
   I read your letter: you however never read mine.

4. Animōs fortēs habētis. Itaque ad hominēs, quī perīculum timent, nāvigāre __dēcrēvistis__. (dēcernere)
   You have brave spirits. So you decided to sail to the people, who fear danger.

5. Saxum nōn __cōnspexī__. Itaque in terram __cecidī__. (cōnspicere, cadere)
   I did not see the stone. So I fell to the ground.

6. Epistulam, quam nautae __mīsērunt__, nōn __vīdī__. (mittere, vidēre)
   I didn't see the letter which the sailors sent.

▶ EXERCISE 5

Change the following sentences so that they are constructed with the dative of possession. The object of each sentence will be the subject in the rewritten sentences. Then translate the rewritten sentences. The Reading Vocabulary may be consulted.

Example: Māgnōs agrōs habeō.
Māgnī mihi sunt agrī.   I have big fields.

1. Avunculus meus nāvēs habēbat.

    Nāvēs avunculō meō erant.

    My uncle had ships.

2. Vīllam, quae est prope montem Vesuvium, habēmus.

    Nōbīs est vīlla, quae est prope montem Vesuvium.

    We have a country house which is near Mount Vesuvius.

3. Nōn habuī hostēs sed multōs amīcōs.

    Nōn mihi fuērunt hostēs sed multī amīcī.

    I did not have enemies, but many friends.

4. Nautae habent epistulam, quam fēmina, quae erat in lītore, mīsit.

    Nautīs est epistula, quam fēmina, quae erat in lītore, mīsit.

    The sailors have the letter, which the woman, who was on the shore, sent.

5. Sum senex, sed corpus forte habeō.

    Sum senex, sed corpus forte mihi est.

    I am an old man, but I have a strong body.

6. Multās vīllās in vestrīs agrīs habētis.

    Vōbīs sunt multae vīllae in vestrīs agrīs.

    You have many country houses in your fields.

The famous mosaic of a dog, found during the excavation of Pompeii, with the Latin words *Cavē Canem* or "Beware of the Dog."

► EXERCISE 6

The following passage is a ghost story adapted from another letter by Pliny the Younger (Book 7.27), in which he describes a supernatural event that happened in Athens. Translate the following passage into English. New vocabulary is listed below the passage.

Erat Athēnīs māgna domus sed īnfāmis. Noctū ibi audiēbātur vinculōrum sonus. Deinde cōnspiciēbātur fōrma terribilis. Erat senex macer et squālidus. Capillus ēius horrēbat. Vincula gerēbat. Multī, quī in eō aedificiō habitābant, mortuī inveniēbantur. Nēmō causam clādis intellēxit. Tandem domus est dēserta: sōlum id mōnstrum ibi habitābat. Athēnodōrus, philosophus, causam malī intellegere cupīvit. Ibi noctū manēre dēcrēvit. Omnia tunc erant quiēta. Philosophus in tenebrīs manēbat librīsque studēbat. Tunc sonum audīvit vinculōrum. Erat autem Athēnodōrō animus fortis. Philosophus oculōs in librōs intendit, nec mōnstrum cōnspexit, quod ad eum appropinquāvit. Tandem fōrmam mōnstrī terribilem vīdit. Senex macer et squālidus digitō aliquid ostendere vidēbātur, deinde ēvānuit. Postrīdiē philosophus iussit locum effodī, quem umbra senis ostendit. Ibi erant ossa hominis mortuī catēnīs vīncta.

There was at Athens a large house, but of evil repute. There the sound of chains was heard at night. Then a terrible form used to be observed. It was a very emaciated and filthy old man. His hair was sticking straight out. He was carrying chains. Many who lived in that building used to be found dead. No one understood the reason for this disaster. At last the house was deserted. Only that apparition lived there. Athenodorus, a philosopher, wanted to understand the reason for the evil. He decided to stay there at night. Everything then was quiet. The philosopher waited in the shadows and studied his books. Then he heard the sound of chains. Athenodorus had a brave spirit. The philosopher concentrated his eyes on his books, and he did not look at the monster, which approached him. At last he saw the terrible shape of the apparition. The emaciated and filthy old man seemed to show something with his finger, then he vanished. On the next day the philosopher ordered the place to be dug up, which the ghost of the old man showed. There were the bones of a dead man bound by chains.

aedificium, aedificiī, n. – building
aliquid – something
appropinquō, appropinquāre, appropinquāvī, appropinquātum – to approach
Athēnīs – in Athens
Athēnodōrus, Athēnodōrī, m. – Athenodorus
capillus, capillī, m. – hair
catēna, catēnae, f. – chain
dēsertus, dēserta, dēsertum – deserted
domus, domūs, f. – house
effodiō, effodere, effōdī, effossum – to dig up
ēvānēscō, ēvānēscere, ēvānuī, ——— – to vanish
horreō, horrēre, horruī, ——— – to stick straight out
īnfāmis, īnfāme – of evil repute
intendō, intendere, intendī, intentum – to focus on, to concentrate on

inveniō, invenīre, invēnī, inventum – to discover
macer, macra, macrum – emaciated, very thin
mōnstrum, mōnstrī, n. – monster, apparition
mortuus, mortua, mortuum – dead
nēmō (nominative) – no one
noctū (adv.) – at night
os, ossis, n. – bone
philosophus, philosophī, m. – philosopher
postrīdiē (adv.) – on the next day
quiētus, quiēta, quiētum – quiet
sōlus, sōla, sōlum – only, alone
sonus, sonī, m. – sound
squālidus, squālida, squālidum – filthy
terribilis, terribile – terrible, fearful
umbra, umbrae, f. – shadow, ghost
vīnctus, vīncta, vīnctum – bound

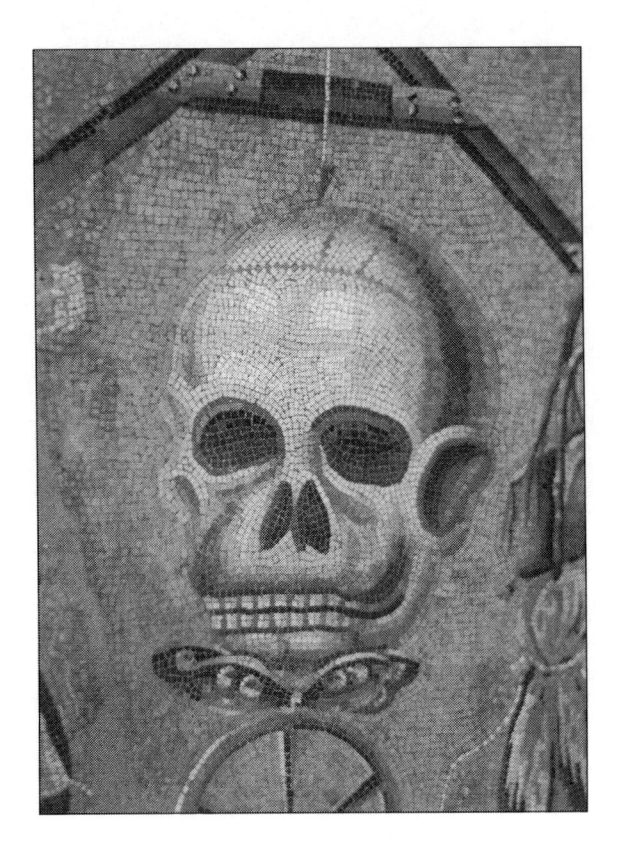

This mosaic of a skull, found in Pompeii, is shown hanging from a plumb line which in turn hangs from a carpenter's level. On one side of the skull (not seen in this photograph) is purple material and a sceptre, which both represent wealth and power. On the other side (cut off in this photograph) is rough material and a beggar's sack, both representing poverty. This balancing of the skull between symbols of wealth and poverty is a reminder that all people, from all walks of life, die. The butterfly and the wheel below the skull represent the fleeting nature of human life.

CONTENT QUESTIONS

After completing Chapter 16, answer these questions.

1. What was Pliny the Younger's position and what are his best known writings?
   Pliny the Younger was an imperial administrator and he is best known for his collection of letters.

2. Who was Pliny's uncle?
   Pliny's uncle was a commander in the imperial navy and the author of a treatise on natural history.

3. From what principal part of each verb is the perfect tense formed?
   The third principal part.

4. What are the two meanings of the perfect tense?
   The perfect tense either refers to a time completed in the past, or an event that happens just before the present.

5. Is there any difference in the endings of the perfect active tense for each conjugation?
   The endings of the perfect active tense are the same for all conjugations.

6. What two ways to express possession have been studied in this chapter?
   We can express possession either with the verb *habeō*, or with dative of possession. In the latter situation, the person possessing is expressed by the dative and the thing possessed is in the nominative case. The verb is always a form of *esse*.

CHAPTER 17

▶ EXERCISE 1
Decline the following phrases.

1. *impetus māgnus*

	Singular	**Plural**
Nominative	impetus māgnus	impetūs māgnī
Genitive	impetūs māgnī	impetuum māgnōrum
Dative	impetuī māgnō	impetibus māgnīs
Accusative	impetum māgnum	impetūs māgnōs
Ablative	impetū māgnō	impetibus māgnīs
Vocative	impetus māgne	impetūs māgnī

2. *gelū (frost)/ācre*

	Singular	**Plural**
Nominative	gelū ācre	gelua ācria
Genitive	gelūs ācris	geluum ācrium
Dative	gelū ācrī	gelibus ācribus
Accusative	gelū ācre	gelua ācria
Ablative	gelū ācrī	gelibus ācribus
Vocative	gelū ācre	gelua ācria

▶ EXERCISE 2
Conjugate the following verbs in the pluperfect active and translate each form.

1. *currō, currere, cucurrī, cursum*

Pluperfect Active: *currō*

	Singular		Plural	
First person	cucurreram	I had run	cucurrerāmus	we had run
Second person	cucurrerās	you had run	cucurrerātis	you had run
Third person	cucurrerat	s/he/it had run	cucurrerant	they had run

2. *iaciō, iacere, iēcī, iactum*

Pluperfect Active: *iaciō*

	Singular		Plural	
First person	iēceram	I had thrown	iēcerāmus	we had thrown
Second person	iēcerās	you had thrown	iēcerātis	you had thrown
Third person	iēcerat	s/he/it had thrown	iēcerant	they had thrown

3. dēvastō, dēvastāre, dēvastāvī, dēvastātum

Pluperfect Active: *dēvastō*

	Singular		Plural	
First person	dēvastāveram	I had devastated	dēvastāverāmus	we had devastated
Second person	dēvastāverās	you had devastated	dēvastāverātis	you had devastated
Third person	dēvastāverat	s/he/it had devastated	dēvastāverant	they had devastated

▶ EXERCISE 3

Translate the Latin into English and the English into Latin.

1. potuerātis — you (pl.) had been able
2. fuerāmus — we had been
3. corripuerāmus — we had seized
4. you had tried — temptāverās
5. iēcerat — s/he/it had thrown
6. you (plural) had lost — āmīserātis
7. exstīnxerant — they had extinguished
8. alueram — I had nourished
9. you (plural) had run — cucurrerātis
10. you had been — fuerās

The following three exercises are based on the works of the historian Suetonius (ca. 70–150 CE) who lived somewhat later than Tacitus and is less famous than Tacitus. The imperial bureaucracy was a major institution in his day, and his works reflect this condition. He wrote *Dē vītā Caesarum* (*On the lives of the emperors*), biographies of the emperors between Caesar and Domitian, and *Dē virīs illūstribus* (*On famous men*), biographies of Roman poets, historians, and rhetors. Suetonius' lives of the emperors make entertaining reading. He loves gossip, and likes to dwell on unsavory details of their personal lives. It is interesting that even in the case of emperors whom Suetonius presumably admired he makes no attempt to whitewash their characters. He presents their achievements and faults equally. Suetonius follows certain patterns: for example, he regularly recounts a person's last words. He exposes facts without historical judgment. His work strongly influenced the tradition of medieval biography.

TIMELINE:

44 BCE–murder of Iūlius Caesar
27 BCE–14 CE emperor Augustus
14 CE–37 CE emperor Tiberius
37 CE–41 CE emperor Caligula
41 CE–54 CE emperor Claudius
54 CE–68 CE emperor Nerō

The assassins rush at and kill Julius Caesar on the Ides of March, 44 BCE.

▶ EXERCISE 4

Translate the following text into English.

Deī dīxerant Caesarī Īdūs Mārtiās eī allātūrās esse clādem. Īdibus Mārtiīs Caesar in senātum intrāvit et dīxit: "Īdūs Mārtiae iam vēnērunt, sed clādēs nōn vēnit." Tunc homō Caesarī respondit: "Īdūs Mārtiae fortasse iam vēnērunt, sed nōndum discessērunt." Mox hominēs Caesarem gladiīs occīdērunt. Caesar vīdit inter eōs esse amīcum suum Brūtum et ante mortem exclāmāvit: "Et tū, Brute!"

The gods had told Caesar that the Ides of March would bring him a disaster. On the Ides of March Caesar entered

the senate and said: "The Ides of March have already come, but the disaster has not come." Then a man replied to

Caesar: "The Ides of March maybe have already come, but have not yet gone away." Soon people killed Caesar with

swords. Caesar saw that his friend Brutus was among them and before (his) death exclaimed: "And you, Brutus!"

allātūrās esse (future infinitive) – would bring
Brūtus, Brūtī, m. – Brutus
Caesar, Caesaris, m. – Caesar
exclāmō, exclāmāre, exclāmāvī, exclāmātum – to exclaim
Īdūs, Īduum, f. pl. – Ides (the 13th or the 15th day of every month);
   Īdibus Mārtiīs – on the Ides of March, i.e., on March 15th

inter + accusative – among
Mārtius, Mārtia, Mārtium – belonging to the month of March
nōndum (adv.) – not yet
senātus, senātūs, m. – senate

The teacher may mention that in Suetonius' version Caesar exclaims more emotionally "And you also, my child!" The exclamation with Brutus' name in it is found in Shakespeare's *Julius Caesar*.

Tiberius Caesar Augustus, second Julio-Claudian emperor of Rome.

▶ EXERCISE 5

Translate the following text into Latin.

The emperor Augustus had already departed from life. The new emperor was Tiberius. Everything was in confusion. People had to show tears because of the death of the emperor and joy because of the new emperor. Then everybody had to swear that they desired always to obey the emperor and to have only that freedom which the emperor had given.

Augustus imperātor iam ex vītā discesserat. Novus imperātor erat Tiberius. Omnia erant in tumultū. Hōminēs dēbēbant lacrimās ostendere propter imperātōris mortem et gaudium propter novum imperātōrem. Tum omnēs iūrāre dēbēbant sē cupere semper imperātōrī obtemperāre et sōlum eam lībertātem habēre quam imperātor dederat.

Augustus, Augustī, m. – Augustus
iūrō, iūrāre, iūrāvī, iūrātum – to swear, to take an oath
lībertās, lībertātis, f. – freedom
obtemperō, obtemperāre, obtemperāvī, obtemperātum
   + dative – to obey someone

sōlum (adv.) – only
Tiberius, Tiberiī, m. – Tiberius

Bust of the third Julio-Claudian emperor Gāius Caligula.

▶ EXERCISE 6

Translate the following text into English.

Caligula semper temptābat pecūniam ex Rōmānīs corripere. Multī hominēs, quī timēbant, Caligulam hērēdem suum nuncupāverant. Sī eī vīvere pergēbant, imperātor fortī īrā capiēbātur et putābat eōs esse dērīsōrēs. Itaque eīs cuppēdiās, quās venēnāverat, mittere solēbat.

Caligula always tried to seize money from the Romans. Many people, who were afraid, had nominated

Caligula their heir. If they continued to live, the emperor was seized by a strong anger and thought that

they were mockers. And so he was accustomed to send them cakes which he had poisoned.

Caligula, Caligulae, m. – Caligula
cuppēdiae, cuppēdiārum, f. pl. – dainty dishes, delicacies
dērīsor, dērīsōris, m. – mocker
hērēs, hērēdis, m. – heir
nuncupō, nuncupāre, nuncupāvī, nuncupātum – to nominate

pecūnia, pecūniae, f. – money
pergō, pergere, perrēxī, perrēctum – to continue
sī – if
venēnō, venēnāre, venēnāvī, venēnātum – to poison

CONTENT QUESTIONS

After completing Chapter 17, answer these questions.

1. The pluperfect endings for all conjugations look like what other verb tense?
   The imperfect indicative of *sum*.

2. How do you translate the pluperfect?
   "Had" + verb.

3. What is the characteristic vowel in the fourth declension?
   The characteristic vowel is *-u*.

4. In which case do the neuter nouns of the fourth declension have a different ending from the masculine and feminine nouns (besides the nominative, the accusative, and the vocative)?
   Dative singular: *cornū* versus *tumultuī*.

5. What is the subject of Tacitus' "Dialogue about the Orators"?
   About the decline of eloquence in imperial times.

6. When was the great fire in Rome? What caused it?
   64 CE. The cause is uncertain. It may have been caused by the emperor Nero.

CHAPTER 18

▶ EXERCISE 1

Conjugate the following verbs in the future perfect active and translate each form.

1. *excitō, excitāre, excitāvī, excitātum*

Future Perfect Active: *excitō*

Singular

First person	excitāverō	I will/shall have awakened
Second person	excitāveris	you will have awakened
Third person	excitāverit	s/he/it will have awakened

Plural

First person	excitāverimus	we will/shall have awakened
Second person	excitāveritis	you will have awakened
Third person	excitāverint	they will have awakened

2. *mittō, mittere, mīsī, missum*

Future Perfect Active: *mittō*

Singular

First person	mīserō	I will/shall have sent
Second person	mīseris	you will have sent
Third person	mīserit	s/he/it will have sent

Plural

First person	mīserimus	we will/shall have sent
Second person	mīseritis	you will have sent
Third person	mīserint	they will have sent

3. *fugiō, fugere, fūgī, ——*

Future Perfect Active: *fugiō*

Singular

First person	fūgerō	I will/shall have fled
Second person	fūgeris	you will have fled
Third person	fūgerit	s/he/it will have fled

Plural

First person	fūgerimus	we will/shall have fled
Second person	fūgeritis	you will have fled
Third person	fūgerint	they will have fled

▶ EXERCISE 2

Decline the following phrase.

The teacher may mention the modern expression bonā fidē, "in good faith."

1. bona fidēs (fidēs, fideī, f. – faith)

	Singular	Plural
Nominative	bona fidēs	bonae fidēs
Genitive	bonae fideī	bonārum fidērum
Dative	bonae fideī	bonīs fidēbus
Accusative	bonam fidem	bonās fidēs
Ablative	bonā fidē	bonīs fidēbus
Vocative	bona fidēs	bonae fidēs

▶ EXERCISE 3

Fill in the blanks with the correct form of the verb in parentheses and translate the completed sentence.

Example: Sī ___potueris___ ad mē venīre, māgnum gaudium habēbō. (possum)
If you can come to me, I will have great joy.

1. Cum epistulam meam ___lēgeris___, ad eam respondēre dēbēbis. (legō)
   After you read my letter, you will have to answer it.

2. Sī uxor marītum ___cōnspexerit___, amor eam corripiet. (cōnspiciō)
   If the wife looks at the husband, love will seize her.

3. Sī fāta ___scīverimus___, timēbimusne? (sciō)
   If we know the fates, will/shall we fear?

4. Cum eum tumultum ___vīderis___, fugiēs. (videō)
   When you see this uproar, you will run.

5. Cum domum ___intrāverimus___, dormiēmus. (intrō)
   When we go into/enter the house, we will/shall sleep.

▶ EXERCISE 4

Translate into Latin.

1. Wait for the day! — Diem exspectā!
2. I kept reading for many days. — Per multōs diēs legēbam.
3. These faces are renowned (famous). — Eae faciēs sunt celebrēs.
4. We will eat at midday (*use a simple ablative*). — Merīdiē comedēmus.
5. With what things did you (plural) give us help? — Quibus rēbus auxilium nōbīs dedistis?
6. I am eager for good things. — Bonīs rēbus studeō.

The Roman author Petronius, who lived at the time of the emperor Nero (ca. 27–66 CE), is the author of another novel-like work, which is in some respects similar to Apuleius' *Golden Ass*. Its title is *Satyricon*, a satiric prose account (intertwined with some poetry) of the adventures of a group of friends in southern Italy. Only fragments of the *Satyricon* still survive, though many of these fragments are quite large.

Petronius was Nero's adviser and, because of his taste for sophistication, called *arbiter ēlegantiārum* ("judge of refinement"). Nero had a habit of turning against friends, many of whom he suspected of sedition or plotting against him. Petronius too became the object of the emperor's anger and he was ordered to commit suicide. Before his death Petronius lampooned the emperor in his will. A copy was sent to Nero.

Such mixture of poetry and prose is called Menippean satire (after the name of the third century BCE Greek author Menippus, who first used this mixed genre.)

Romans reclining at a lavish banquet while slaves serve food and entertainment is being offered.

▶ EXERCISE 5

In the sentences below, you will see a partial description of the famous *Cēna Trimalchiōnis*, "Trimalchio's dinner," a lavish dinner-party described in *Satyricon*. In this exercise, your viewpoint is that of someone who has already attended similar parties and predicts what will happen at this one. Combine each pair of simple sentences into one complex sentence containing a *cum*-clause. Use the appropriate verb tense. Then translate the newly formed sentence. The adverb *posteā* will disappear in the complex sentence. Use the appropriate verb tense and translate the newly formed sentence.

Example: Ad casam veniētis. Posteā intrābitis.
Cum ad casam vēneritis, intrābitis.
When you come to the cottage, you will come in.

1. Servī aquam dabunt. Posteā manūs lavābitis.
    lavō, lavāre, lāvī, lōtum – to wash   servus, servī, m. – slave

    Cum servī aquam dederint, manūs lavābitis.

    When the slaves bring water, you (pl.) will wash hands.

2. Manūs lavābitis. Posteā gustātiōnem māgnam habēbitis.
    gustātiō, gustātiōnis, f. – appetizer

    Cum manūs lāveritis, gustātiōnem māgnam habēbitis.

    After you (pl.) wash hands, you (pl.) will have a large appetizer.

3. Gustātiōnem māgnam habēbitis. Posteā ōva comedētis.
    ōvum, ōvī, n. – egg

    Cum gustātiōnem māgnam habueritis, ōva comedētis.

    After you have a great appetizer, you will eat eggs.

4. Ōva comedētis. Posteā vīnum bibētis.
   bibō, bibere, bibī, ——— – to drink   vīnum, vīnī, n. – wine

   Cum ōva comēderitis, vīnum bibētis.

   After you (pl.) eat eggs, you (pl.) will drink wine.

5. Vīnum bibētis. Posteā leporem comedētis.
   lepus, leporis, m. – rabbit

   Cum vīnum biberitis, leporem comedētis.

   After you (pl.) drink wine, you (pl.) will eat a rabbit.

6. Leporem comedētis. Posteā servī aprum vōbīs pōnent.
   aper, aprī, m. – boar

   Cum leporem comēderitis, servī aprum vōbīs pōnent.

   After you (pl.) eat a rabbit, the slaves will serve you (literally "place for you") a boar.

7. Servī aprum vōbīs pōnent. Posteā fābulās nārrābitis.

   Cum servī aprum vōbīs posuerint, fābulās nārrābitis.

   After the slaves serve you a boar, you (pl.) will tell stories.

These types of amphoras and other vessels might have been used to serve and store food and beverages.

▶ EXERCISE 6

The following text, adapted from *Satyricon*, is a story of the type called "Milesian tale": a funny short story featuring love and adventure. Translate the following text into English.

Mulier marītum suum āmīserat et dē eō valdē dolēbat. Corpus marītī, quod in conditōriō iacēbat, tenēbat et lacrimīs cōnsūmēbātur. Propter dolōrem vidua nōn comēdēbat nec dormīre cupiēbat. Prope conditōrium erant trēs latrōnēs crucifīxī, quōrum corpora ā mīlite custōdiēbantur. Mīles vīdit rem in conditōriō movērī et in conditōrium intrāvit. Tunc mulierem cōnspexit et putāvit eam esse mōnstrum. Deinde tamen intellēxit eam esse uxōrem quae dē marītō mortuō dolēbat et cōnsūmēbātur. Tum inquit: "Cibum comedere dēbēs. Sī cibum nōn comēderis, tū quoque mox nōn vīvēs." Cēnam suam dare eī cupiēbat. Fēmina prīmum recūsābat, sed tandem accēpit. Nōn sōlum cibōs comēdit, sed ūnā cum mīlite rīdēbat. Dum mīles cum muliere manēbat, familiārēs ūnīus latrōnis crucifīxī ēius corpus clam corripuērunt. Mīles pūnīrī dēbēbat; nam nōn bene custōdīverat. Vidua nōn cupiēbat suum amīcum pūnīrī. Itaque corpus marītī mortuī eī dedit, quod mīles in locum corporis ablātī posuit. Hominēs id crēdere nōn poterant.

A woman had lost her husband and was feeling very much grief concerning him. She was holding the body of the husband, which was lying in the funeral chamber, and was consumed by tears. Because of grief the widow was not eating and she did not wish to sleep. Close to the funeral chamber there were three crucified bandits whose bodies were being guarded by a soldier. The soldier saw that a thing (something) was moving in the funeral chamber and entered it. Then he saw the woman and thought that she was an apparition. However, afterwards <he> understood that she was a wife who was grieving about her dead husband and being consumed <by grief>. Then he said: "You need to eat food. If you do not eat food, you also soon will not live." <He> wished to give her his dinner. The woman refused at first, but at last she accepted. <She> not only ate foods, but also laughed with the soldier. While the soldier remained with the woman, the relatives of one <dead> criminal secretly snatched his body. The soldier had to be punished; for he had not guarded well. The widow did not wish her friend to be punished. So she gave him the body of the dead husband, which the soldier put in place of the body <which had been> taken away. People were unable to believe it.

---

ablātus, ablāta, ablātum – taken away
accipiō, accipere, accēpī, acceptum – to accept
cēna, cēnae, f. – dinner
cibus, cibī, m. – food
clam (adv.) – secretly
conditōrium, conditōriī, n. – funeral chamber
crucifīxus, crucifīxa, crucifīxum – crucified
custōdiō, custōdīre, custōdīvī, custōdītum – to guard
familiārēs, familiārium, m. pl. – family members
latrō, latrōnis, m. – criminal, bandit

mōnstrum, mōnstrī, n. – monster, apparition
mortuus, mortua, mortuum – dead
prīmum (adv.) – at first
pūniō, pūnīre, pūnīvī, pūnītum – to punish
recūsō, recūsāre, recūsāvī, recūsātum – to refuse
reveniō, revenīre, revēnī, reventum – to return
rīdeō, rīdēre, rīsī, rīsum – to laugh
trēs (nominative masculine) – three
ūnīus – genitive singular of *ūnus*
vidua, viduae, f. – widow

The name of this type of story is taken from the city of Miletus in Asia Minor, which was the birthplace of the first author of such stories.

CONTENT QUESTIONS

After completing Chapter 18, answer these questions.

1. What new feature appears in the Latin literature in the second century CE?
   Archaism, a taste for rare or obsolete words and expressions from early Latin.

2. Who are the three "wise" emperors?
   Hadrian, Antoninus Pius, Marcus Aurelius.

3. What is unique about Apuleius' *Golden Ass*?
   It is the only complete example of fiction in Latin to survive from the Roman period.

4. To what forms are the endings of the future perfect very similar?
   To the future of *sum*.

5. What is the usual gender of the nouns belonging to the fifth declension?
   Feminine.

6. What is the characteristic vowel of the nouns of the fifth declension?
   -e-

CHAPTER 19

▶ EXERCISE 1

Decline the following phrases.

1. *haec barba*

	Singular	Plural
Nominative	haec barba	hae barbae
Genitive	hūius barbae	hārum barbārum
Dative	huic barbae	hīs barbīs
Accusative	hanc barbam	hās barbās
Ablative	hāc barbā	hīs barbīs

2. *hoc proelium*

	Singular	Plural
Nominative	hoc proelium	haec proelia
Genitive	hūius proeliī	hōrum proeliōrum
Dative	huic proeliō	hīs proeliīs
Accusative	hoc proelium	haec proelia
Ablative	hōc proeliō	hīs proeliīs

▶ EXERCISE 2

Conjugate the following verbs in the perfect passive and translate each form.

1. *sānō, sānāre, sānāvī, sānātum*

Perfect Passive: *sānō*

Singular

First person	sānātus, sānāta, (sānātum) sum	I was healed, have been healed
Second person	sānātus, sānāta, (sānātum) es	you were healed, have been healed
Third person	sānātus, sānāta, sānātum est	s/he/it was healed, has been healed

Plural

First person	sānātī, sānātae, (sānāta) sumus	we were healed, have been healed
Second person	sānātī, sānātae, (sānāta) estis	you were healed, have been healed
Third person	sānātī, sānātae, sānāta sunt	they were healed, have been healed

2. *dūcō, dūcere, dūxī, ductum*

Perfect Passive: *dūcō*

Singular

First person	ductus, ducta, (ductum) sum	I was led, have been led
Second person	ductus, ducta, (ductum) es	you were led, have been led
Third person	ductus, ducta, ductum est	s/he/it was led, has been led

Plural

First person	ductī, ductae, (ducta) sumus	we were led, have been led
Second person	ductī, ductae, (ducta) estis	you were led, have been led
Third person	ductī, ductae, ducta sunt	they were led, have been led

▶ EXERCISE 3

Fill in the blanks in the following sentences with the correct form of the perfect passive participle of the verbs whose infinitives are in parentheses. Translate each sentence, once using the longer literal translation and a second time using the shortened literal translation.

Example: In vulneribus ___sānātīs___ cicātrīcēs manent. (sānāre)
The scars stay on the wounds having been healed.   The scars stay on the healed wounds.

1. In epistulā ___missā___ nōn multa verba sunt. (mittere)
   There are not many words in the letter having been sent.
   There are not many words in the sent letter.

2. Fortitūdō Germānōrum ___relictōrum___ manēbat. (relinquere)
   Germānus, Germānī, m. – German
   The courage of the Germans having been left behind remained.
   The courage of the Germans left behind remained.

3. Casās ab Hūnīs ___aedificātās___ nōn vidēmus. (aedificāre)
   Hūnus, Hūnī, m. – Hun
   We do not see dwellings having been built by the Huns.
   We do not see dwellings built by the Huns.

4. Mīlitēs Germānōrum ad bellum ___parātōs___ nōn timēmus. (parāre)
   We do not fear the soldiers of the Germans having been prepared for a war.
   We do not fear the soldiers of the Germans prepared for a war.

5. Fēminae ā Rōmānīs ___captae___, deinde ___līberātae___ ad Germānōs fūgērunt. (capere) (līberāre)
   The women having been captured by the Romans, then having been freed, fled to the Germans.
   The women captured by the Romans, then freed, fled to the Germans.

6. Suntne haec vestīmenta mīlitum ___vulnerātōrum___? (vulnerāre)
   Are these the clothes of the soldiers having been wounded?
   Are these the clothes of the wounded soldiers?

The Huns are pictured marching through Gaul, plundering this Roman province.

▶ EXERCISE 4

Fill in the blanks in the following sentences with the correct form of the demonstrative pronoun/adjective *hic, haec, hoc*. Translate the sentences.

Example: ___Haec___ cōnsilia semper audiuntur.
These counsels/plans are always heard.

1. In ___hīs___ equīs semper manent Hūnī.
   The Huns always stay on these horses.

2. Dē ___hāc___ herbā nihil scīmus.
   We know nothing about this plant.

3. ___Hōrum___ hominum māgnam fortitūdinem vidēmus.
   We see the great courage of these people.

4. Hoc est ___hūius___ fēminae cōnsilium novum.
   This is the new counsel/plan of this woman.

5. In ___hāc___ nūbe nihil vidērī potest.
   In this cloud nothing can be seen.

6. ___Hae___ herbae captae sunt ex agrīs.
   These plants have been taken from the fields.

7. ___Huic___ rēgīnae praeclārae dōna dabimus.
   We shall give gifts to this distinguished queen.

Attila and the Huns were master horsemen. Here you see the Huns on horseback attacking. Attila and the Huns drove the Roman emperor Valentinian III from Ravenna in 452 CE. Although he reached Rome, Attila did not invade the city.

▶ EXERCISE 5

Change the perfect active verb into the perfect passive. Use the ablative of agent or instrument in the changed sentences where needed. Then translate the changed sentence.

Example: Herbās ex hīs agrīs cēpimus.
Herbae ex hīs agrīs ā nōbīs captae sunt.   The plants were/have been taken from these fields by us.

1. Dē Hūnīs nōn multa audīvimus.

   Dē Hūnīs nōn multa ā nōbīs sunt audīta.

   Not many things about the Huns were/have been heard by us.

2. Germānī mīlitēs fēminārum cōnsilia exspectāvērunt.

   Fēminārum cōnsilia ā Germānīs mīlitibus sunt exspectāta.

   The counsels/plans of the women were/have been awaited by the German soldiers.

3. Vōs, amīcī, saepe vocāvī.

   Estis, amīcī, saepe ā mē vocātī.

   Friends, you were/have often been called by me.

4. Ducēs nōs hanc urbem capere iussērunt.

   Iussī ā ducibus sumus hanc urbem capere.

   We were/have been ordered by the generals to take this city.

5. Hanc carnem numquam coximus.

   Haec carō numquam ā nōbīs est cocta.

   This meat has never been cooked by us/was never cooked by us.

6. Castra Hūnōrum cōnspeximus.

   Castra Hūnōrum ā nōbīs sunt cōnspecta.

   The camp of the Huns was/has been observed by us.

▶ EXERCISE 6

Translate the following questions. Then choose the best answer for each and translate. The Reading Vocabulary may be consulted.

1. Cūr Hūnī nōn sōlum gladiōs sed etiam laqueōs in proeliō habent?

    Hūnī laqueīs et gladiīs pugnant.

    Hūnī hostēs laqueīs occidere solent.

    Nōn est iīs difficile hostēs laqueīs captōs gladiīs occīdere.

    Why do the Huns have not only swords, but also lassos in battle?

    Nōn est eīs difficile hostēs laqueīs captōs gladiīs occīdere.

    It is not difficult for them to kill with <their> swords enemies having been captured by lassos.

2. Ubi (*where*) habitant Hūnī?

    Hūnī casās habent.

    Hūnī forīs vīvunt.

    Hūnī ubīque terribilēs vidērī cupiunt.

    In what place do the Huns dwell?

    Hunī forīs vīvunt.

    The Huns live outdoors.

3. Quās rēs in equīs faciunt Hūnī?

    In equīs comedunt, in equīs dormiunt, in equīs pugnant.

    Sine equīs Hūnī impetūs in hostēs facere solent.

    Hūnī saepe ab equīs sēparantur.

    What things do the Huns do on their horses?

    In equīs comedunt, in equīs dormiunt, in equīs pugnant.

    They eat on their horses, they sleep on their horses, they fight on their horses.

4. Solentne Hūnī carnem coquere?

    Carō ā Hūnīs nōn comeditur.

    Hūnī vestīmenta ex animālium pellibus facta gerunt.

    Carō ā Hūnīs nōn coquitur, sed paulisper teritur.

    Are the Huns accustomed to cook meat?

    Carō ā Hūnīs nōn coquitur, sed paulisper teritur.

    Meat is not cooked by the Huns, but rubbed for a little while.

5. Ubi crēscunt herbae, quārum rādīcēs comedere solent Hūnī?

> Herbae, quārum rādīcēs comedere solent Hūnī, in agrīs cōnspiciuntur.
>
> Hūnī rādīcēs herbārum et animālium carnem comedere solent.
>
> Hūnī vestīmenta ex animālium pellibus facta gerunt.

Where do the plants grow, whose roots the Huns are accustomed to eat?

Herbae, quārum rādīcēs comedere solent Hūnī, in agrīs cōnspiciuntur.

The plants, whose roots the Huns are accustomed to eat, are observed in fields.

6. Cūr Hūnī terribilēs vidērī timōremque in aliīs hominibus excitāre cupiunt?

> Faciēs Hūnōrum cōnsultō vulnerantur.
>
> Hūnī pulchram fōrmam habēre cupiunt.
>
> Hūnī sunt hominēs ferī et ferōcēs.

Why do the Huns want to appear terrifying and stir up fear in other people?

Hūnī sunt hominēs ferī et ferōcēs.

The Huns are wild and ferocious people.

Attila the Hun lived from 406 to 453 CE. As Khan of the Huns, he was the leader of the Hunnic Empire. He was known for his ferocity and savagery.

CONTENT QUESTIONS

After completing Chapter 19, answer these questions.

1. How does the participle behave both like a verb and an adjective?
   It has a tense, voice, and number like a verb, as well as case, number, and gender like an adjective.

2. What part of the speech is *hic, haec, hoc*?
   Demonstrative pronoun and demonstrative adjective.

3. How is the perfect passive indicative of any verb formed?
   The perfect passive participle plus the forms of *sum* as an auxiliary verb.

4. Ammianus Marcellinus wrote his history as a continuation of the work of which historian?
   As a continuation to the *Histories* of Tacitus.

5. What were the effects of the movements of the Huns in the third and fourth centuries CE?
   Other peoples, especially Germanic tribes, while fleeing the Huns, were pushed west into the Roman empire.

6. When did the Huns themselves enter the Roman empire?
   In the mid-fifth century CE.

CHAPTER 20

▶ EXERCISE 1

Conjugate the following verbs in the pluperfect passive and translate each form.

1. *pūniō, pūnīre, pūnīvī, pūnītum*

Pluperfect Passive: *pūniō*

Singular

First person	pūnītus, pūnīta, (pūnītum) eram	I had been punished
Second person	pūnītus, pūnīta, (pūnītum) erās	you had been punished
Third person	pūnītus, pūnīta, pūnītum erat	s/he/it had been punished

Plural

First person	pūnītī, pūnītae, (pūnīta) erāmus	we had been punished
Second person	pūnītī, pūnītae, (pūnīta) erātis	you had been punished
Third person	pūnītī, pūnītae, pūnīta erant	they had been punished

2. *dēlectō, dēlectāre, dēlectāvī, dēlectātum*

Pluperfect Passive: *dēlectō*

Singular

First person	dēlectātus, dēlectāta, (dēlectātum) eram	I had been pleased
Second person	dēlectātus, dēlectāta, (dēlectātum) erās	you had been pleased
Third person	dēlectātus, dēlectāta, dēlectātum erat	s/he/it had been pleased

Plural

First person	dēlectātī, dēlectātae, (dēlectāta) erāmus	we had been pleased
Second person	dēlectātī, dēlectātae, (dēlectāta) erātis	you had been pleased
Third person	dēlectātī, dēlectātae, dēlectāta erant	they had been pleased

▶ EXERCISE 2

Decline the following phrases.

1. *ille fūr*

	Singular	**Plural**
Nominative	ille fūr	illī fūrēs
Genitive	illīus fūris	illōrum fūrum
Dative	illī fūrī	illīs fūribus
Accusative	illum fūrem	illōs fūrēs
Ablative	illō fūre	illīs fūribus

2. *illud fūrtum*

	Singular	**Plural**
Nominative	illud fūrtum	illa fūrta
Genitive	illīus fūrtī	illōrum fūrtōrum
Dative	illī fūrtō	illīs fūrtīs
Accusative	illud fūrtum	illa fūrta
Ablative	illō fūrtō	illīs fūrtīs

▶ EXERCISE 3

Change the following sentences from the active to the passive voice and translate the revised sentence.

Example: Dolor mē corripuerat.
Dolōre eram correptus/-a.
I had been seized by pain.

1. Aequō animō illās rēs tolerāveram.
   tolerō, tolerāre, tolerāvī, tolerātum – to tolerate

   Illae rēs aequō animō ā mē erant tolerātae.

   Those things had been tolerated by me with indifference.

2. Pauperēs omnia āmīserant.

   Omnia ā pauperibus erant āmissa.

   Everything had been lost by the poor people.

3. Liber ille dē rēbus hūmānīs et dīvīnīs nōs docuerat.

   Dē rēbus hūmānīs et dīvīnīs nōs librō illō erāmus doctī.

   We had been taught about human and divine things by that book.

4. Urbēs timōris plēnās vīderātis.

   Urbēs timōris plēnae ā vōbīs erant vīsae.

   Cities full of fear had been seen by you.

▶ EXERCISE 4

Fill in the blanks with the correct perfect infinitive using the verb in parentheses. Translate the sentences.

Example: Augustīnus nārrat sē nōn bonum adulēscentem ___fuisse___. (esse)
Augustine tells that he was not a good young man.

1. Augustīnus tamen dīcit sē propter fūrtum nōn ___esse pūnītum___. (pūniō)
   Augustine says, however, that he was not punished because of the theft.

2. Augustīnus intellēxit rēs malās ā sē ___esse factās___. (faciō)
   Augustine understood that bad things had been done by him.

3. Augustīnus sciēbat sē nōn ___dēbuisse___ pōma aliōrum hominum capere. (dēbeō)
   Augustine knew that he should not have taken the fruits of other people.

4. Augustīnus intellēxit adulēscentēs pōma capta nōn ___dēlectāvisse___. (dēlectō)
   Augustine understood that the stolen (taken) fruits had not pleased the young men.

5. Augustīnus dīcit sē et suōs amīcōs rēs malās facere ___cupīvisse___. (cupiō)
   Augustine says that he and his friends desired to do bad things.

Aurēlius Augustīnus, known as Augustine,
bishop of Hippo, seated here with a child
named Adeodatus, perhaps his son,
next to him.

▶ EXERCISE 5

Translate into Latin.

1. Augustine had sought the tree with his friends during the night.
   Augustīnus, Augustīnī, m. – Augustine

   Augustīnus arborem cum suīs amīcīs noctū quaesīverat.

2. The tree had been sought by Augustine and his friends during the night.

   Arbor ab Augustīnō et ab ēius amīcīs noctū erat quaesīta.

3. The young men had done many bad things.

   Adulēscentēs multa mala fēcerant.

4. Many bad things had been done by the young men.

   Multa mala ab adulēscentibus erant facta.

5. They had left all the fruits.

   Omnia pōma relīquerant.

6. All the fruits had been left by them.

   Omnia pōma ab eīs erant relicta.

▶ EXERCISE 6

Translate the following passage into English. It has been adapted from Augustine's *Confessions*.

Litterās Graecās nōn valdē amābam. Nam litterīs Latīnīs puer eram alitus et eās amāveram. Verba tamen Graeca difficilia mihi vidēbantur. Ex litterīs Latīnīs meminī mē maximē esse dēlectātum dē Aeneā et dē Dīdōne legere. Legēbam Aeneam rēgīnam relīquisse et ad Ītaliam nāvigāvisse et dolēbam. Legēbam omnia misera Dīdōnī esse vīsa et eam sē occīdisse et dolēbam. Illa fābula animum meum semper movēbat et eā dēlectābar. Sed dē vītā meā nōn cōgitābam nec cōgitābam mē dēbēre rēs bonās quaerere et bonum esse. Putō illīs temporibus mē potuisse tantum dē librīs Latīnīs cōgitāre.

I did not love/like Greek literature very much. For as a boy I had been nourished by Latin literature and had loved/liked it. However, the Greek words seemed to me difficult. From Latin literature I remember that I was especially pleased to read about Aeneas and Dido. I used to read that Aeneas had left the queen and had sailed to Italy, and I used to feel pain. I used to read that everything had seemed wretched to Dido and that she had killed herself, and I used feel pain. That story always moved my mind and I was delighted with it. But I did not think about my life and I did not think that I had to seek good things and to be good. I think that in those times I could only think about Latin books.

Aenēās, Aenēae, m. – Aeneas
Dīdō, Dīdōnis, f. – Dido
Graecus, Graeca, Graecum – Greek
Ītalia, Ītaliae, f. – Italy

Latīnus, Latīna, Latīnum – Latin
maximē (adv.) – especially
meminī – <I> remember

Dido is reclining on a couch across from Aeneas.

CONTENT QUESTIONS

After completing Chapter 20, answer these questions.

1. What are Augustine's *Confessions* about?
   They are his spiritual autobiography.

2. Where was Augustine born?
   North Africa.

3. In what way are the perfect and pluperfect passive indicatives similar, and in what way are they different?
   Both are formed with the perfect passive participle; the perfect passive indicative is formed with the present of *sum*, and the pluperfect passive indicative is formed with the imperfect of *sum*.

4. How are the perfect active and the perfect passive infinitives different in appearance?
   The perfect active infinitive is a single word, while the perfect passive infinitive is formed with a perfect passive participle and the infinitive of *sum*.

5. Where are the perfect infinitives mainly used?
   In the accusative and infinitive construction.

6. What are the differences in the meaning of *hic, haec, hoc* and *ille, illa, illud*?
   Hic, haec, hoc means "this" and indicates a close person or thing, while *ille, illa, illud* means "that" and indicates a far person or thing. When a series of persons or things has been mentioned, *ille* means "former" and *hic* "latter."

7. What is the dual use of *hic, haec, hoc* and *ille, illa, illud*?
   They can be used both as pronouns (by themselves) and as adjectives (with another noun).

CHAPTER 21

▶ EXERCISE 1

Conjugate the following verbs in the future perfect passive and translate each form.

1. *accipiō, accipere, accēpī, acceptum*

Future Perfect Passive: *accipiō*

Singular

First person	acceptus, accepta, (acceptum) erō	I will have been received
Second person	acceptus, accepta, (acceptum) eris	you will have been received
Third person	acceptus, accepta, acceptum erit	s/he/it will have been received

Plural

First person	acceptī, acceptae, (accepta) erimus	we will have been received
Second person	acceptī, acceptae, (accepta) eritis	you will have been received
Third person	acceptī, acceptae, accepta erunt	they will have been received

2. *accūsō, accusāre, accusāvī, accusātum*

Future Perfect Passive: *accūsō*

Singular

First person	accūsātus, accūsāta, (accūsātum) erō	I will have been accused
Second person	accūsātus, accūsāta, (accūsātum) eris	you will have been accused
Third person	accūsātus, accūsāta, accūsātum erit	s/he/it will have been accused

Plural

First person	accūsātī, accūsātae, (accūsāta) erimus	we will have been accused
Second person	accūsātī, accūsātae, (accūsāta) eritis	you will have been accused
Third person	accūsātī, accūsātae, accūsāta erunt	they will have been accused

▶ EXERCISE 2

Decline the future active participle of the following verb.

1. tollō, tollere, sustulī, sublātum

Singular

	Masculine	Feminine	Neuter
Nominative	sublātūrus	sublātūra	sublātūrum
Genitive	sublātūrī	sublātūrae	sublātūrī
Dative	sublātūrō	sublātūrae	sublātūrō
Accusative	sublātūrum	sublātūram	sublātūrum
Ablative	sublātūrō	sublātūrā	sublātūrō
Vocative	sublātūre	sublātūra	sublātūrum

Plural

	Masculine	Feminine	Neuter
Nominative	sublātūrī	sublātūrae	sublātūra
Genitive	sublātūrōrum	sublātūrārum	sublātūrōrum
Dative	sublātūrīs	sublātūrīs	sublātūrīs
Accusative	sublātūrōs	sublātūrās	sublātūra
Ablative	sublātūrīs	sublātūrīs	sublātūrīs
Vocative	sublātūrī	sublātūrae	sublātūra

▶ EXERCISE 3

Translate into Latin.

1. The wheel will have been turned.
   Rota versāta erit.

2. You (plural) will have descended.
   Dēscenderitis.

3. We will have been rebuked.
   Reprehēnsī erimus.

4. You (singular) will have rebuked.
   Reprehenderis.

5. S/he will have raised up her/his hand.
   Manum suam sustulerit.

6. You (plural) will have been raised up.
   Sublātī eritis.

7. Nothing will have been changed.
   Nihil mūtātum erit.

8. I will have changed many things.
   Multa/multās rēs mūtāverō.

9. The rewards will have been snatched away.
   Praemia ērepta erunt.

10. These men will have snatched away the rewards.
    Hī hominēs praemia ēripuerint.

▶ EXERCISE 4

Change the infinitives in the following indirect statements into future infinitives and translate the changed sentences.

Example: Tē multās rēs ā mē accipere crēdō.
Tē multās rēs ā mē acceptūrum/am esse crēdō.
I believe that you will receive many things from me.

1. Nōn multōs hominēs dīvitiās et honōrēs habēre scīmus.
   Nōn multōs hominēs dīvitiās et honōrēs habitūrōs esse scīmus.
   We know that not many men will have riches and honors.

2. Amīcī meī Fortūnam multa mihi dare sed mē nihil possidēre dīcēbant.
   Amīcī meī Fortūnam multa mihi datūram esse sed mē nihil possessūrum/am esse dīcēbant.
   My friends used to say that Fortune would give me many things, but that I would possess nothing.

3. Fortūna cōnstantiam sē nōn amāre dīxit.
   Fortūna cōnstantiam sē nōn amātūram esse dīxit.
   Fortune said that she would not like constancy.

4. Cīvēs animālia sua prope urbem manēre dīxērunt.
   Cīvēs animālia sua prope urbem mānsūra esse dīxērunt.
   The citizens said that their animals would remain near the city.

5. Rēgīna sorōrem suam discēdere nōn putat.
   Rēgīna sorōrem suam discessūram esse nōn putat.
   The queen does not think that her sister is going to depart.

6. Odium numquam esse bonum dīcō.
   Odium numquam futūrum esse bonum dīcō.
   I say that hatred will never be good.

▶ EXERCISE 5

Translate into Latin.

1. On the point of receiving wealth and honors we love Fortune.
   Dīvitiās et honōrēs acceptūrī/acceptūrae Fortūnam amāmus.

2. I say that they are going to receive wealth and honors.
   Dīvitiās et honōrēs eōs/eās acceptūrōs/acceptūrās esse dīcō.

3. On the point of making a mistake we have suddenly been changed.
   Errātūrī/errātūrae subitō mūtātī/mūtātae sumus.

4. You (singular) said that they would make a mistake.
   Eōs/eās errātūrōs/errātūrās esse dīxistī.

5. Being about to go down to the sea we observe the ships.
   Ad mare dēscēnsūrī/dēscēnsūrae nāvēs cōnspicimus.

6. Being about to receive gifts they await the queen.
   Dōna acceptūrī/acceptūrae rēgīnam exspectant.

7. We seem to be about to receive gifts.
   Vidēmur dōna acceptūrī/acceptūrae esse.

▶ EXERCISE 6

Translate the following passage into English.

In this passage adapted from his *Cōnsōlātiō philosophiae* (2.7), Boethius criticizes the earlier Roman view that winning glory for great actions was a way of winning a kind of immortality. According to this view, if one did great deeds, especially in the political or military sphere, these deeds would be always remembered by future generations. This view motivated great Roman statesmen, such as Cicero. But Boethius didn't think much of this idea, as we see here. For him, the only immortality that mattered was immortality of the individual soul.

Sī terra nostra cum māgnitūdine tōtīus caelī comparāta erit, vidēbitur esse nihil. Sed terrae pars, in quā habitant hominēs, est valdē parva! In tam parvō spatiō quanta esse potest glōria ūnīus hominis? Et in tam parvō spatiō multae sunt gentēs, multae sunt linguae. Hominēs ūnīus gentis linguās externās nōn saepe intellegunt. Itaque glōria ūnīus hominis ad gentēs externās venīre nōn potest. Sī autem accēperimus glōriam ūnīus hominis in locō valdē parvō mānsūram esse, nec umquam ad gentēs externās ventūram esse, dē tempore quoque cōgitāre dēbēbimus. Sī ūnum temporis pūnctum cum decem mīlibus annōrum comparātum erit, vidēbitur esse nihil. Sī autem decem mīlia annōrum cum tempore īnfīnītō comparāta erunt, vidēbuntur esse nihil. Itaque etiam sī glōria ūnīus hominis per decem mīlia annōrum mānserit, nihil erit. Et glōria, etiam sī per decem mīlia annōrum manēre potuerit, mortālis tandem erit, sicut vīta hominum.

If our earth is compared with the vastness of the whole universe, it will seem to be nothing. But the part of the earth in which men live, is very small! How great can the glory of a single man be in such a small space? And in such a small space there are many nations, there are many languages. Men of one nation do not often understand foreign languages. Therefore the glory of one man cannot come to foreign nations. If, however, we accept that the glory of one person is going to remain in a very small region, and is not ever going to come to external nations, we will also need to think about time. If one point of time is compared with ten thousand years, it will seem to be nothing. If, however, ten thousand years are compared with infinite time, they will seem to be nothing. Therefore, even if the glory of a single person remains through ten thousand years, it will be nothing. And glory, even if it is able to last through ten thousand years, will at last be mortal, just as the life of people.

annus, annī, m. – year
caelum – means also "universe"
comparō, comparāre, comparāvī, comparātum – to compare (with *cum* + ablative)
decem mīlia, mīlium – ten thousand: *decem* has no declensional endings; *mīlia* in the plural is a noun and is joined with the genitive of the word to which it refers
gēns, gentis, f. – race, people, nation
glōria, glōriae, f. – glory

īnfīnītus, īnfīnīta, īnfīnītum – infinite
lingua, linguae, f. – language, tongue
māgnitūdō, māgnitūdinis, f. – vastness, great extent
mortālis, mortāle – mortal, perishable
pūnctum, pūnctī, n. – point
quantus, quanta, quantum – how great?
spatium, spatiī, n. – space
tōtīus – genitive singular of *tōtus, tōta, tōtum* = all, whole
ūnīus – genitive singular of *ūnus, ūna, ūnum* = one, a single

Anicius Manlius Sevērīnus Boēthius, ca. 480–ca. 524 CE.

CONTENT QUESTIONS

After completing Chapter 21, answer these questions.

1. When did Boethius live?
   Just after the fall of the Roman empire in the West.

2. What image from Boethius' *Cōnsōlātiō philosophiae* remained famous for centuries?
   The wheel of Fortune.

3. How is the future perfect passive of all conjugations formed?
   The perfect passive participle with the future indicative of *sum*.

4. How is the future active participle formed?
   Take away the *-um* from the fourth principal part and substitute in its place the ending *-ūrus, -ūra, -ūrum*.

5. How is the future active infinitive formed?
   The nominative singular or plural (or the accusative) of the future active participle with *esse*.

6. What is the approximate English translation of the future active participle?
   "(Being) about to...," or "(being) on the point of...," or "(being) ready to...," or "going to...," or "intending to..."

ENGLISH TO LATIN GLOSSARY

This glossary contains all the **Vocabulary to Learn** from the chapters.

LIST OF ABBREVIATIONS:

(1) = first conjugation
abl. = ablative
acc. = accusative
adj. = adjective
adv. = adverb
conj. = conjunction
dat. = dative

f. = feminine
gen. = genitive
inf. = infinitive
m. = masculine
n. = neuter
pl. = plural
prep. = preposition

NOTE:

The genitive of the words of second declension ending in *–ius* or *–ium* is indicated with a single *ī* which is the ending itself. Note that in the full form there is normally a double *i*: fīlius, ī, i.e., fīliī, gaudium, ī, i.e., gaudiī.

A

abandon, relinquō, -ere, relīquī, relictum
abound with, abundō (1) + *abl.*
about, dē, *prep.* + *abl.*
about to be, futūrus, -a, -um, *participle*
accept, accipiō, -ere, -cēpī, -ceptum
accuse someone of something, accūsō (1) + *acc.* + *gen.*
adopt, capiō, -ere, cēpī, captum
after (conj.), cum, *conj.*; postquam, *conj.*
after (prep.), post, *prep.* + *acc.*
afterwards, posteā, *adv.*
against, contrā, *prep.* + *acc.*
all, omnis, -e, *adj.*
almost, paene, *adv.*
already, iam, *adv.*
also, etiam, *adv.*; quoque, *adv.*
always, semper, *adv.*
among, inter, *prep.* + *acc.*
and, et, *conj.*; atque, *conj.*; -que, *conj.*
and not, nec, *conj.*
and so, itaque, *conj.*
anger, īra, -ae, *f.*
animal, animal, -ālis, *n.*
another, alius, alia, aliud, *adj.*
answer, respondeō, -ēre, -spondī, -spōnsum
any, ūllus, -a, -um, *adj.*
appearance, fōrma, -ae, *f.*
argument, argūmentum, -ī, *n.*
armed, armātus, -a, -um, *adj.*
around, circum, *prep.* + *acc.*
ash, cinis, -eris, *m.*
ask, rogō (1)
at home, domī
at last, tandem, *adv.*
at the house of, apud, *prep.* + *acc.*
athlete, āthlēta, -ae, *m.*
attack, impetus, -ūs, *m.*
await, exspectō (1)
awaken, excitō (1)
away from, ā *or* ab, *prep.* + *abl.*
axis, axle, axis, -is, *m.*

B

bad, malus, -a, -um, *adj.*
battle, proelium, -ī, *n.*
be, sum, esse, fuī, ——
be able, possum, posse, potuī, ——
be accustomed, soleō, -ēre, solitus sum + *inf.*
be afraid, timeō, -ēre, timuī, ——
be eager for, studeō, -ēre, studuī, —— + *dat.*
be inert, iaceō, -ēre, iacuī, ——
be interested in, studeō, -ēre, studuī, —— + *dat.*
be on fire, ārdeō, -ēre, ārsī, ——
be unwilling, nōlō, *irregular verb*
beard, barba, -ae, *f.*
beautiful, pulcher, pulchra, pulchrum, *adj.*
because of, propter, *prep.* + *acc.*
beginning, initium, -ī, *n.*
behave, agō, -ere, ēgī, āctum; **(s/he) behaves,** sē gerit
believe somebody, crēdō, -ere, crēdidī, crēditum + *dat.*
between, inter, *prep.* + *acc.*
blame, reprehendō, -ere, -prehendī, -prehēnsum
blood, sanguis, sanguinis, *m.*
body, corpus, -oris, *n.*
book, liber, librī, *m.*
bosom, gremium, -ī, *n.*
boy, puer, puerī, *m.*
brave, fortis, -e, *adj.*
brook, rīvus, -ī, *m.*
build, aedificō (1)
burn, ārdeō, -ēre, ārsī, ——
but, sed, *conj.*
by, ā *or* ab, *prep.* + *abl.*

C

call, vocō (1)
camp, castra, -ōrum, *n. pl.*
can, possum, posse, potuī, ——
capture, capiō, -ere, cēpī, captum
care for, cūrō (1)
carry, gerō, -ere, gessī, gestum
cause, causa, -ae, *f.*
cave, spēlunca, -ae, *f.*
chain, vinculum, -ī, *n.*
change, mūtō (1)
chest, pectus, -oris, *n.*
choose, legō, -ere, lēgī, lēctum
citizen, cīvis, -is, *m./f.*
city (city of Rome), urbs, urbis, *f.*
clothes, vestīmenta, -ōrum, *n. pl.*
cloud, nūbēs, -is, *f.*
combat, proelium, -ī, *n.*
come, veniō, -īre, vēnī, ventum
concerning, dē, *prep. + abl.*
conflagration, incendium, -ī, *n.*
confusion, tumultus, -ūs, *m.*
consider, putō (1)
constancy, cōnstantia, -ae, *f.*
consul, cōnsul, -ulis, *m.*
consume, cōnsūmō, -ere, -sūmpsī, -sūmptum
cook, coquō, -ere, coxī, coctum
cottage, casa, -ae, *f.*
country house, vīlla, -ae, *f.*
courage, fortitūdō, -inis, *f.*
crowded, celeber, -bris, -bre, *adj.*
cruel, crūdēlis, -e, *adj.*
cultivate, colō, -ere, coluī, cultum

D

danger, perīculum, -ī, *n.*
darkness, tenebrae, -ārum, *f. pl.*
daughter, fīlia, -ae, *f.*
day, diēs, diēī, *m./f.*
deadly, fūnestus, -a, -um, *adj.*
death, mors, mortis, *f.*
deception, dolus, -ī, *m.*
decide, dēcernō, -ere, -crēvī, -crētum + *inf.*
defeat, vincō, -ere, vīcī, victum
delight, dēliciae, -ārum, *f. pl.*
delight, dēlectō (1)

descend, dēscendō, -ere, -scendī, -scēnsum
design, parō (1)
desire, cupiō, -ere, -īvī, -ītum
destiny, fātum, -ī, *n.*
destroy, dēleō, -ēre, dēlēvī, dēlētum; tollō, -ere, sustulī, sublātum
devastate, dēvastō (1)
difficult, difficilis, -e, *adj.*
disaster, clādēs, -is, *f.*
distinguished, praeclārus, -a, -um, *adj.*
divine, dīvīnus, -a, -um, *adj.*
do, agō, -ere, ēgī, āctum; faciō, -ere, fēcī, factum
down from, dē, *prep. + abl.*
drive, agō, -ere, ēgī, āctum
during the night, noctū, *adv.*
dwell, habitō (1)

E

each, omnis, -e, *adj.*
easily, facile, *adv.*
eat, comedō, -ere, -ēdī, -ēsum
emperor, imperātor, -ōris, *m.*
enemy, hostis, -is, *m.*
enter, intrō (1)
envy someone, invideō, -ēre, invīdī, invīsum, + *dat.*
eruption, incendium, -ī, *n.*
esteem, aestimō (1)
even (adj.), aequus, -a, -um, *adj.*
even (adv.), etiam, *adv.*
ever, umquam, *adv.*
every, omnis, -e, *adj.*
everywhere, ubīque, *adv.*
example, exemplar, -āris, *n.*; exemplum, -ī, *n.*
exceedingly, valdē, *adv.*
exclaim, exclāmō (1)
expect, exspectō (1)
external, externus, -a, -um, *adj.*
extinguish, exstinguō, -ere, exstīnxī, exstīnctum
eye, oculus, -ī, *m.*

F

face, faciēs, -ēī, *f.*
fall, cadō, -ere, cecidī, cāsum

family, familia, -ae, *f.*
famous, praeclārus, -a, -um, *adj.*
far, longē, *adv.*
farmer, agricola, -ae, *m.*
fate, fātum, -ī, *n.*
fatherland, patria, -ae, *f.*
fear, timor, -ōris, *m.*
fear, timeō, -ēre, timuī, ——
feed, alō, -ere, aluī, altum/alitum
feel, sentiō, -īre, sēnsī, sēnsum
feel pain, doleō, -ēre, doluī, ——
ferocious, ferōx, -ōcis, *adj.*
fetter, vinculum, -ī, *n.*
few, paucī, -ae, -a, *adj.*
field, ager, agrī, *m.*
fierce, ācer, ācris, ācre, *adj.*; ferōx, -ōcis, *adj.*
fight, pugnō (1)
finger, digitus, -ī, *m.*
fire, ignis, -is, *m.*
first, prīmus, -a, -um, *adj.*
flame, flamma, -ae, *f.*
flee, fugiō, -ere, fūgī, ——
fleet, classis, -is, *f.*
flesh, carō, carnis, *f.*
flow, fluō, -ere, flūxī, fluxum
for (conj.), enim, *conj.*; nam, *conj.*
for (prep.), prō, *prep. + abl.*
for a long time, diū, *adv.*
for certain, for sure, prō certō, *adverbial phrase*
force, vīs, ——, *f., pl.* vīrēs, vīrium; impetus, -ūs, *m.*
foreign to, aliēnus, -a, -um, *adj. + prep.* ā/ab + *abl.*
forest, silva, -ae, *f.*
form, fōrma, -ae, *f.*
fortunate, fēlīx, -īcis, *adj.*
fortune, fortitūdō, -inis, *f.*
Fortune, the goddess Fortūna, -ae, *f.*
free someone from something, līberō (1), + *acc.* + *abl.*
friend, amīcus, -ī, *m.*
from, ā *or* ab, *prep. + abl.*; ē *or* ex, *prep. + abl.*
fruit, pōmum, -ī, *n.*
full of, plēnus, -a, -um, *adj. + gen.* or + *abl.*

G

garment, vestīmentum, -ī, *n.*
general, dux, ducis, *m.*
geographical places, loca, locōrum, *n. pl.*
get ready, parō (1)
gift, dōnum, -ī, *n.*
girl, puella, -ae, *f.*
give, dō, dăre, dedī, dătum
go to, petō, -ere, petīvī, petītum
god, deus, -ī, *m.*
goddess, dea, -ae, *f.*
good, bonus, -a, -um, *adj.*
goodbye!, valē!
great, māgnus, -a, -um, *adj.*
grief, dolor, -ōris, *m.*
grow, crēscō, -ere, crēvī, ——

H

hand, manus, -ūs, *f.*
happy, fēlīx, -īcis, *adj.*
hatred, odium, -ī, *n.*
have, habeō, -ēre, habuī, habitum
head, caput, -itis, *n.*
head for, petō, -ere, petīvī, petītum
heal, sānō (1)
hear, audiō, -īre, audīvī, audītum
heart, cor, cordis, *n.*
heaven, caelum, -ī, *n.*
help, auxilium, -ī, *n.*
her, suus, -a, -um, *possessive adj.,* ēius
herself, sē, *acc. of the reflexive pronoun*
hide, pellis, -is, *f.*
hide, occultō (1)
himself, sē, *acc. of the reflexive pronoun*
his, suus, -a, -um, *possessive adj.,* ēius
hold, teneō, -ēre, tenuī, tentum
home, domus, -ūs, *f.*
honor, honor, -ōris, *m.*
horn, cornū, -ūs, *n.*
horse, equus, -ī, *m.*
house, domus, -ūs, *f.*
household, familia, -ae, *f.*
however, autem, *conj.;* tamen, *conj.*
human, hūmānus, -a, -um, *adj.*
hurt, doleō, -ēre, doluī, ——, *(intransitive)*
husband, marītus, -ī, *m.*

I

I, ego, *personal pronoun*
I do not care a bit, aestimō ūnīus assis
if, sī, *conj.*
immediately, statim, *adv.*
impetus, impetus, -ūs, *m.*
important, māgnus, -a, -um
in, in, *prep. + abl.*
in fact, enim, *conj.;* nam, *conj.*
in front of, ante, *prep. + acc.*
in such a way, ita, *adv.*
in the open, forīs, *adv.*
inconsistent with, aliēnus, -a, -um, *adj. + prep.* ā/ab *+ abl.*
indication, argūmentum, -ī, *n.*
indifferently, aequō animō
injustice, inīquitās, -ātis, *f.*
into, ad, *prep. + acc.;* in, *prep. + acc.*
it is allowed to, it is permitted (for someone to do something) licet + *dat. + inf.*
its, suus, -a, -um, *possessive adj.,* ēius
itself, sē, *acc. of the reflexive pronoun*

J

joy, gaudium, -ī, *n.*
judge, iudex, -icis, *m.*
judge, iūdicō (1)
just, iūstus, -a, -um, *adj.*
just as, sīcut, *adv.*

K

keen, ācer, ācris, ācre, *adj.*
kill, occīdō, -ere, occīdī, occīsum
king, rēx, rēgis, *m.*
know, sciō, scīre, scīvī, scītum

L

lack something, egeō, -ēre, eguī, —— *+ abl.*
land, terra, -ae, *f.*
lap, gremium, -ī, *n.*
large, māgnus, -a, -um, *adj.*
latter, hic, haec, hoc
law, lēx, lēgis, *f.*
lead, agō, -ere, ēgī, āctum; dūcō, -ere, dūxī, ductum
leader, dux, ducis, *m.*
learned, doctus, -a, -um, *adj.*
leave, discēdō, -ere, -cessī, -cessum
leave behind, relinquō, -ere, relīquī, relictum
legitimate, iūstus, -a, -um, *adj.*
letter (epistle), litterae, -ārum, *f. pl.;* epistula, -ae, *f.*
letter (of the alphabet), littera, -ae, *f.*
lie down, iaceō, -ēre, iacuī, ——
life, vīta, -ae, *f.*
lift up, tollō, -ere, sustulī, sublātum
like, similis, -e, *adj. + gen.* or *+ dat.*
listen, audiō, -īre, -īvī, -ītum
literature, litterae, -ārum, *f. pl.*
little house, casa, -ae, *f.*
live (be alive), vīvō, -ere, vīxī, vīctum
live (dwell), habitō (1)
long, longus, -a, -um, *adj.*
look at, cōnspiciō, -ere, -spexī, -spectum
look for, quaerō, -ere, quaesīvī, quaesītum
look here!, ecce, *interj.*
lose, āmittō, -ere, -mīsī, -missum
love, amor, -ōris, *m.*
love, amō (1)

M

make, faciō, -ere, fēcī, factum
make a mistake, errō (1)
make a speech, ōrātiōnem habeō
make plans, cōnsilia capiō
man, vir, virī, *m.*
man (i.e., human being), homō, -inis, *m.*
many, multus, -a, -um, *adj.*
matter, rēs, reī, *f.*
meat, carō, carnis, *f.*
meet, conveniō, -īre, -vēnī, -ventum
memory, memoria, -ae, *f.*
midday, merīdiēs, -ēī, *m.*
mind, animus, -ī, *m.*
mistress, domina, -ae, *f.*
mother, māter, mātris, *f.*
mountain, mōns, montis, *m.*
mouth, ōs, ōris, *n.*
move, moveō, -ēre, mōvī, mōtum
much, multus, -a, -um, *adj.*
much, multum, *adv.*
must, dēbeō, -ēre, dēbuī, dēbitum *+ inf.*
my, meus, -a, -um, *possessive adj.*

N

name, nōmen, -inis, *n.*
near, prope, *prep. + acc.*
neglect, neglegō, -ere, neglēxī, neglēctum
never, numquam, *adv.*
new, novus, -a, -um, *adj.*
nice, pulcher, pulchra, pulchrum, *adj.*
night, nox, noctis, *f.*
no, minimē, *adv.*
nor, nec, *conj.*
not, nōn, *negative adv.*
not only . . . , but also . . . , nōn sōlum . . . , sed etiam . . .
not want, nōlō, *irregular verb*
nothing, nihil, *negative pronoun*
nourish, alō, -ere, aluī, altum/alitum
now, nunc, *adv.*

O

observe, cōnspiciō, -ere, -spexī, -spectum
often, saepe, *adv.*
old, vetustus, -a, -um, *adj.*
old age, senectūs, -ūtis, *f.*
old man, senex, -is, *m.*
on, in, *prep. + abl.*
on account of, propter, *prep. + acc.*
on behalf of, prō, *prep. + abl.*
only, tantum, *adv.*
oracle, ōrāculum, -ī, *n.*
order, iussus, -ūs, *m.*
order somebody to do something, iubeō, -ēre, iussī, iussum + *acc. + inf.*
other, alius, alia, aliud, *adj.*
ought, dēbeō, -ēre, dēbuī, dēbitum + *inf.*
our, noster, nostra, nostrum, *possessive adj.*
out of, ē *or* ex, *prep. + abl.*
outside, forīs, *adv.*
outward, externus, -a, -um, *adj.*
overcome, vincō, -ere, vīcī, victum
overwhelm, opprimō, -ere, oppressī, oppressum
owe, dēbeō, -ēre, dēbuī, dēbitum

P

pain, dolor, -ōris, *m.*
parent, parēns, parentis, *m./f.*
part, pars, partis, *f.*
particle added to the first word of an interrogative sentence, -ne
passages of a book, locī, locōrum, *m. pl.*
peace, pāx, pācis, *f.*
people, hominēs, hominum, *m. pl.*
perhaps, fortasse, *adv.*
pet, dēliciae, -ārum, *f. pl.*
place, locus, locī, *m.*
place, pōnō, -ere, posuī, positum
plan, cōnsilium, -ī, *n.*
plant, herba, -ae, *f.*
play, lūdō, -ere, lūsī, lūsum
please, dēlectō (1)
poet, poēta, -ae, *m.*
poison, venēnum, -ī, *n.*
poor, pauper, pauperis, *adj.*
possess, possideō, -ēre, possēdī, possessum
prepare, parō (1)
preserve, servō (1)
proof, argūmentum, -ī, *n.*
public office or distinction, honor, -ōris, *m.*
punish, pūniō, -īre, pūnīvī, pūnītum
put, pōnō, -ere, posuī, positum

Q

queen, rēgīna, -ae, *f.*

R

raise, tollō, -ere, sustulī, sublātum
read, legō, -ere, lēgī, lēctum
reason, causa, -ae, *f.*
rebuke, reprehendō, -ere, -prehendī, -prehēnsum
receive, accipiō, -ere, -cēpī, -ceptum
red, ruber, rubra, rubrum, *adj.*
regard, aestimō (1)
remain, maneō, -ēre, mānsī, mānsum
renowned, celeber, -bris, -bre, *adj.*
reward, praemium, -ī, *n.*
rich, dīves, dīvitis, *adj.*
riches, dīvitiae, -ārum, *f. pl.*
right hand, dextra, -ae, *f.*
road, via, -ae, *f.*
rock, saxum, -ī, *n.*
Roman, Rōmānus, -a, -um, *adj.*
Rome, Rōma, -ae, *f.*
rouse, excitō (1)
rub, terō, -ere, trīvī, trītum
run, currō, -ere, cucurrī, cursum
run away, fugiō, -ere, fūgī, ——
rural, rūsticus, -a, -um, *adj.*
rush at, petō, -ere, petīvī, petītum
rustic, rūsticus, -a, -um, *adj.*

S

s/he/it, is, ea, id, *personal pronoun*
sail, nāvigō (1)
sailor, nauta, -ae, *m.*
save, servō (1)
say, dīcō, -ere, dīxī, dictum
say/said, inquam, (*only introducing direct speech*); **s/he says/said,** inquit, (*only introducing direct speech*)
sea, mare, maris, *n.*
search, quaerō, -ere, quaesīvī, quaesītum
see, videō, -ēre, vīdī, vīsum
seek, petō, -ere, petīvī, petītum
seem, videor
seize, corripiō, -ere, -ripuī, -reptum
send, mittō, -ere, mīsī, missum
separate, sēparō (1)
serious, sevērus, -a, -um, *adj.*
severe, sevērus, -a, -um, *adj.*
shadows, tenebrae, -ārum, *f. pl.*
she-wolf, lupa, -ae, *f.*
ship, nāvis, -is, *f.*
shore, lītus, -oris, *n.*
should, dēbeō, -ēre, dēbuī, dēbitum + *inf.*
show, ostendō, -ere, ostendī, ostentum
similar, similis, -e, *adj. + gen.* or + *dat.*
sister, soror, -ōris, *f.*
sit, sedeō, -ēre, sēdī, sessum
skin, pellis, -is, *f.*
sky, caelum, -ī, *n.*
sleep, somnus, -ī, *m.*
sleep, dormiō, -īre, dormīvī, dormītum
small, parvus, -a, -um, *adj.*
smoke, fūmus, -ī, *m.*
snatch away, ēripiō, -ere, -ripuī, -reptum
so great, tantus, -a, -um, *adj.*
so, tam, *adv.*
soldier, mīles, -itis, *m.*
son, fīlius, -ī, *m.*

soon, mox, *adv.*
soul, animus, -ī, *m.*
sparrow, passer, -eris, *m.*
speech, ōrātiō, -ōnis, *f.*
spirit, animus, -ī, *m.*
stand, stō, -āre, stetī, statum
stir up, excitō (1)
stone, saxum, -ī, *n.*
storm, tempestās, -ātis, *f.*
story, fābula, -ae, *f.*
stream, rīvus, -ī, *m.*
strength, vīs, ——, *f., pl.* vīrēs, vīrium
strengthen, firmō (1)
strict, sevērus, -a, -um, *adj.*
strong, fortis, -e, *adj.*
study, studeō, -ēre, studuī, —— + *dat.*
suddenly, subitō, *adv.*
suppress, opprimō, -ere, oppressī, oppressum
swiftly, celeriter, *adv.*
sword, gladius, -ī, *m.*

T

take, capiō, -ere, cēpī, captum; dūcō, -ere, dūxī, ductum
take back, recipiō, -ere, -cēpī, -ceptum
take care of, cūrō (1)
teach, doceō, -ēre, docuī, doctum
tear, lacrima, -ae, *f.*
tell, nārrō (1)
temple, templum, -ī, *n.*
terrifying, terribilis, -e, *adj.*
that, ille, illa, illud, *demonstrative pronoun and adj.*; is, ea, id, *demonstrative pronoun and adj.*
that, quī, quae, quod, *relative pronoun*
theft, fūrtum, -ī, *n.*
their, suus, -a, -um, *possessive adj.*; eōrum, *pronoun*
themselves, sē, *acc. of the reflexive pronoun*
then, deinde, *adv.*; tum, *adv.*; tunc, *adv.*
there, ibi, *adv.*
therefore, igitur, *conj.*

thief, fūr, fūris, *m.*
thing, rēs, reī, *f.*
think, cōgitō (1); putō (1)
this, hic, haec, hoc, *demonstrative pronoun and adj.*; is, ea, id, *demonstrative pronoun and adj.*
through, per, *prep. + acc.*
throw, iaciō, -ere, iēcī, iactum
time, tempus, -oris, *n.*
to, ad, *prep. + acc.*; in, *prep. + acc.*
together, ūnā, *adv.*
touch, tangō, -ere, tetigī, tāctum
towards, ad, *prep. + acc.*
tree, arbor, -oris, *f.*
trickery, dolus, -ī, *m.*
true, vērus, -a, -um, *adj.*
try, temptō (1)
turn, versō (1)

U

uncle, avunculus, -ī, *m.*
understand, intellegō, -ere, intellēxī, intellēctum
uproar, tumultus, -ūs, *m.*

V

vegetation, herba, -ae, *f.*
very, valdē, *adv.*
villa, vīlla, -ae, *f.*
voyage, nāvigō (1)

W

wage war, bellum gerō
wait for, exspectō (1)
wake up, excitō (1)
walk, ambulō (1)
wall, wall-fence, mūrus, -ī, *m.*
wander, errō (1)
want, cupiō, -ere, -īvī, -ītum
war, bellum, -ī, *n.*
water, aqua, -ae, *f.*
we, nōs, *personal pronoun*
wealth, dīvitiae, -ārum, *f. pl.*

weapons, arma, -ōrum, *n.pl.*
wear out, terō, -ere, trīvī, trītum
weather, caelum, -ī, *n.*
well, bene, *adv.*
well-known, celeber, -bris, -bre, *adj.*
what?, quid?, *interrogative pronoun;* quod?, *interrogative adj.*
wheel, rota, -ae, *f.*
when, cum, *conj.*
which, quī, quae, quod, *relative pronoun*
which?, quī, quae, quod?, *interrogative adjective*
while, dum, *conj.*
white, albus, -a, -um, *adj.*
who, quī, quae, quod, *relative pronoun*
who?, quis?, *interrogative pronoun*
why, cūr, *adj.*
wife, uxor, -ōris, *f.*
wind, ventus, -ī, *m.*
with, cum, *prep. + abl.*
with all one's might, prō vīribus
with me, mēcum
with you, tēcum
without, sine, *prep. + abl.*
wolf, *see* she-wolf
woman, fēmina, -ae, *f.*; mulier, -ieris, *f.*
word, verbum, -ī, *n.*
worship, colō, -ere, coluī, cultum
wound, vulnus, -eris, *n.*
wound, vulnerō (1)
wretched, miser, -a, -um, *adj.*

Y

yes, ita, *adv.*
you (pl.), vōs, *personal pronoun*
you (sg.), tū, *personal pronoun*
young lady, young man, adulēscēns, -entis, *m./f.*
your, yours (pl.), vester, vestra, vestrum, *possessive adj.*
your, yours (sg.), tuus, -a, -um, *possessive adj.*

LATIN TO ENGLISH GLOSSARY

This glossary contains the **Vocabulary to Learn*** as well as the **Reading Vocabulary** from all the chapters.

*All words from the **Vocabulary to Learn** are starred and coded, e.g., C12 means the word first appeared as **Vocabulary to Learn** in Chapter 12. In a very few instances, an additional meaning for the word is given in a later part of the text. Such additional meanings appear in the Glossary and when the additional meaning is part of the **Vocabulary to Learn**, the chapter introducing that additional meaning is also noted.

LIST OF ABBREVIATIONS:

(1) = first conjugation
abl. = ablative
acc. = accusative
adj. = adjective
adv. = adverb
conj. = conjunction
dat. = dative
f. = feminine

gen. = genitive
inf. = infinitive
m. = masculine
n. = neuter
pl. = plural
prep. = preposition
sg. = singular

NOTE:

The genitive of second declension words ending in **-ius** or **-ium** is indicated with a single **-ī**, which is the genitive ending itself. Note that in the full form of the genitive there is normally a double *i*: *fīlius, -ī* (= *fīliī*); *gaudium, -ī* (= *gaudiī*).

A

ā *or* **ab,** *prep.* + *abl.*, by, from, away from* C5

absum, abesse, āfuī, ——, to be absent, away

abundō (1) + *abl.*, to abound with* C20

accipiō, -ere, -cēpī, -ceptum, to accept, receive* C21

accurrō, -ere, -currī, -cursum, to run up

accūsō (1) + *acc.* + *gen.*, to accuse someone of something* C21

ācer, ācris, ācre, *adj.*, keen, fierce* C10

ad tempus, for the time being, for a while

ad, *prep.* + *acc.*, towards, to, into* C4

adolēscō, -ere, adolēvī, adultum, to grow up

adulēscēns, -entis, *m./f.,* young man, young lady* C20

aedificō (1), to build* C10

Aenēās, Aenēae (*gen.*), **Aenēae** (*dat.*), **Aenēam/ān** (*acc.*), **Aenēā** (*abl.*), Aeneas, Trojan refugee, legendary founder of Roman race

aequus, -a, -um, *adj.,* even; **aequō animō,** indifferently* C20

Aeschinus, -ī, *m.,* Aeschinus

aestimō (1), to regard, esteem; **aestimō ūnīus assis,** I do not care a bit* C7

ager, agrī, *m.,* field* C3

agō, -ere, ēgī, āctum, to drive, lead, do, behave* C11

agricola, -ae, *m.,* farmer* C1

albus, -a, -um, *adj.,* white* C14

aliēnus, -a, -um, *adj.* + *prep.* ā/ab + *abl.,* foreign to, inconsistent with* C21

alius, alia, aliud, *adj.,* another, other* C13

alō, -ere, aluī, altum/alitum, to feed, nourish* C17

amāns, amantis, *m./f.,* lover

ambulō (1), to walk* C2

amīcus, -ī, *m.,* friend* C3

āmittō, -ere, -mīsī, -missum, to lose* C17

amō (1), to love* C2

amor, -ōris, *m.,* love* C7

Amūlius, -ī, *m.,* Amulius

angustus, -a, -um, *adj.,* narrow

animal, -ālis, *n.,* animal* C9

animus, -ī, *m.,* spirit, soul, mind* C3

ante, *prep.* + *acc.,* in front of* C15

antequam, *conj.,* before

Apollō, Apollinis, *m.,* Apollo, god of the sun, poetry, light, music

appropinquō (1), to approach

apud, *prep.* + *acc.,* at the house of* C13

aqua, -ae, *f.,* water* C1

arbor, -oris, *f.,* tree C14

ārdeō, -ēre, ārsī, ——, to burn, be on fire* C11

argūmentum, -ī, *n.,* proof, indication, argument* C15

arma, -ōrum, *n. pl.,* weapons* C9

armātus, -a, -um, *adj.,* armed* C4

asportō (1), to carry away
at, *conj.*, but
Athēniēnsēs, Athēniēnsium, *m. pl.*, the Athenians
āthlēta, -ae, *m.*, athlete* C1
atque, *conj.*, and* C13
attonitus, -a, -um, *adj.*, astounded
auctōritās, -ātis, *f.*, authority
audiō, -īre, audīvī, audītum, to hear, listen* C9
autem, *conj.*, however* C4
auxilium, -ī, *n.*, help* C5
avunculus, -ī, *m.*, uncle* C16
axis, -is, *m.*, axle, axis* C21

B

barba, -ae, *f.*, beard* C19
bellum, -ī, *n.*, war* C4; **bellō iūstō**, through open warfare
belua, -ae, *f.*, beast
bene, *adv.*, well* C1
bonus, -a, -um, *adj.*, good* C4
bracchium, -ī, *n.*, arm

C

cadō, -ere, cecidī, cāsum, to fall* C14
caelum, -ī, *n.*, sky, heaven, weather* C16
calidus, -a, -um, *adj.*, hot
callidus, -a, -um, *adj.*, clever, cunning
capiō, -ere, cēpī, captum, to take, adopt, capture; **cōnsilia capere**, to make plans* C10
caput, -itis, *n.*, head* C9
carō, carnis, *f.*, meat, flesh* C19
Carthāgine, at Carthage, in Carthage
Carthāgō, -inis, *f.* Carthage
casa, -ae, *f.*, little house, cottage* C3
castra, -ōrum, *n. pl.*, camp* C4
Catilīna, -ae, *m.*, Catiline, a bankrupt revolutionary whose plot to overthrow the republic was exposed by Cicero
Catullus, -ī, *m.*, Catullus, Roman poet
causa, -ae, *f.*, cause, reason* C16
celeber, -bris, -bre, *adj.*, renowned, well-known, crowded* C10
celeriter, *adv.*, swiftly* C19
cibus, -ī, *m.*, food

cicātrīx, cicātrīcis, *f.*, scar
cinis, -eris, *m.*, ash* C16
circum, *prep. + acc.*, around* C21
circus, -ī, *m.*, circus, often referring to the Circus Maximus in particular
cīvis, -is, *m./f.*, citizen* C9
clādēs, -is, *f.*, disaster* C16
clam, *adv.*, secretly
clāmor, -ōris, *m.*, shout, cry
classis, -is, *f.*, fleet* C16
claudō, -ere, clausī, clausum, to lock up
clīvus, -ī, *m.*, hill
cōgitō (1), to think* C5
cōgnōscō, -ere, -nōvī, -nitum, to recognize, get to know
colō, -ere, coluī, cultum, to worship, cultivate* C18
comedō, -ere, -ēdī, -ēsum, to eat* C14
coniūrātiō, -ōnis, *f.*, plot
cōnsilium, -ī, *n.*, plan* C5
cōnspiciō, -ere, -spexī, -spectum, to look at, observe* C11
cōnstantia, -ae, *f.*, constancy* C21
cōnsul, -ulis, *m.*, consul* C9
cōnsultō, *adv.*, on purpose
cōnsūmō, -ere, -sūmpsī, -sūmptum, to consume* C12
contrā, *prep. + acc.*, against* C8
conveniō, -īre, -vēnī, -ventum, to meet* C14
coquō, -ere, coxī, coctum, to cook* C19
cor, cordis, *n.*, heart* C20
cornū, -ūs, *n.*, horn* C17
corpus, -oris, *n.*, body* C9
corripiō, -ere, -ripuī, -reptum, to seize* C17
crēdō, -ere, crēdidī, crēditum + *dat.*, to believe somebody* C9
crēscō, -ere, crēvī, ——, to grow* C19
crūdēlis, -e, *adj.*, cruel* C11
Ctēsiphō, -ōnis, *m.*, Ctesipho
cum ... tum ..., both ... and ...
cum, *conj.*, when, after* C18
cum, *prep. + abl.*, with* C3
Cupīdō, Cupīdinis, *m.*, Cupid (in Greek, Eros)
cupiō, -ere, -īvī, -ītum, to desire, want* C10

cūr, *adv.*, why?* C15
cūria, -ae, *f.*, senate (building)
cūrō (1), to care for, take care of* C2
currō, -ere, cucurrī, cursum, to run* C17

D

dē, *prep. + abl.*, about, concerning, down from* C5
dea, -ae, *f.*, goddess* C18
dēbeō, -ēre, dēbuī, dēbitum + *inf.*, ought, must, should; to owe* C2
dēcernō, -ere, -crēvī, -crētum + *inf.*, to decide, determine* C8
deinde, *adv.*, then* C3
dēlectō (1), to delight, please* C20
dēleō, -ēre, dēlēvī, dēlētum, to destroy* C10
dēliciae, -ārum, *f. pl.*, delight, pet
dēliciae, -ārum, *f. pl.*, delight, pet* C7
Delphicus, -a, -um, *adj.*, belonging to Delphi, Delphic
Delphīs, at Delphi
Dēmea, -ae, *m.*, Demea
dēns, dentis, *m.*, tooth
dēscendō, -ere, -scendī, -scēnsum, to descend* C21
deus, -ī, *m.*, god* C10
dēvastō (1), to devastate* C17
dextra, -ae, *f.*, right hand* C12
dīcō, -ere, dīxī, dictum, to say* C8
Dīdō, Dīdōnis, *f.*, Dido, exile from Phoenician Tyre, founding queen of Carthage
diēs, diēī, *m./f.*, day* C18
difficilis, -e, *adj.*, difficult* C15
digitus, -ī, *m.*, finger* C7
discēdō, -ere, -cessī, -cessum, to leave* C13
discō, -ere, didicī, ——, to learn
diū, *adv.*, for a long time* C2
dīves, dīvitis, *adj.*, rich* C13
dīvīnus, -a, -um, *adj.*, divine* C20
dīvitiae, -ārum, *f. pl.*, wealth, riches* C21
dō, dăre, dedī, dătum, to give* C4
doceō, -ēre, docuī, doctum, to teach* C5
doctus, -a, -um, *adj.*, learned* C13
doleō, -ēre, doluī, ——, to feel pain, hurt* C5

dolor, -ōris, *m.,* grief, pain* C11
dolus, -ī, *m.,* trickery, deception* C4
domī, at home* C3
domina, -ae, *f.,* mistress* C7
domus, -ūs, *f.,* house, home* C17
dōnum, -ī, *n.,* gift* C10
dormiō, -īre, dormīvī, dormītum, to sleep* C18
Druidēs, -um, *m. pl.,* the Druids
dūcō, -ere, dūxī, ductum, to lead, take* C13
dulcissime rērum, dear fellow, literally "the sweetest of all things"
dum, *conj.,* while* C6
duo, duae, dua, *numeral,* two
dux, ducis, *m.,* leader, general* C8

E

ē or **ex,** *prep. + abl.,* from, out of* C4
ecce, *interj.,* look here! * C15
egeō, -ēre, eguī, —— *+ abl.,* to lack something* C20
egestās, -ātis, *f.,* lack, poverty
ego, *personal pronoun,* I* C3
ēiciō, -ere, eiēcī, eiectum, to throw away
enim, *conj.,* for, in fact* C13
eō diē, on that day
epistula, -ae, *f.,* letter* C5
equus, -ī, *m.,* horse* C10
ēripiō, -ere, -ripuī, -reptum, to snatch away* C21
errō (1), to wander, make a mistake* C21
et, *conj.,* and* C1
etiam, *adv.,* even, also* C15
Etrūscus, -a, -um, *adj.,* Etruscan
ēvanēscō, -ere, ēvanuī, ——, to disappear
excitō (1), to awaken, wake up, rouse, stir up* C18
exclāmō (1), to exclaim* C18
excutiō, -ere, -cussī, -cussum, to shake off
exemplar, -āris, *n.,* example* C9
exemplum, -ī, *n.,* example* C6
exeunt, they exit, go out
eximō, -ere, -ēmī, -ēmptum, to take out
exspectō (1), to wait for, await, expect* C2

exstinguō, -ere, exstīnxī, exstīnctum, to extinguish* C17
externus, -a, -um, *adj.,* outward, external* C21

F

Fābricius, -ī, *m.,* Fabricius
fābula, -ae, *f.,* story* C2
faciēs, -ēī, *f.,* face* C18
facile, *adv.,* easily* C17
faciō, -ere, fēcī, factum, to do, make* C12
familia, -ae, *f.,* family, household
familia, -ae, *f.,* family, household* C5
fātum, -ī, *n.,* fate, destiny
fātum, -ī, *n.,* fate, destiny* C18
fax, facis, *f.,* torch
Fēlīciō, ——, *m.,* Felicio, a servant's name
fēlīx, -īcis, *adj.,* fortunate, happy* C10
fēmina, -ae, *f.,* woman* C16
femur, femoris, *n.,* the upper leg, the thigh
ferōx, -ōcis, *adj.,* fierce, ferocious* C19
ferus, -a, -um, *adj.,* wild, savage
fīlia, -ae, *f.,* daughter* C1
fīlius, -ī, *m.,* son C3
firmō (1), to strengthen* C6
flamma, -ae, *f.,* flame* C10
flexus, -a, -um, *adj.,* curved
fluō, -ere, flūxī, fluxum, to flow* C14
folium, -ī, *n.,* leaf
forīs, *adv.,* outside, in the open* C19
fōrma, -ae, *f.,* form, appearance* C2
fortasse, *adv.,* perhaps* C15
fortis, -e, *adj.,* brave, strong* C10
fortitūdō, -inis, *f.,* courage* C8
fortūna, -ae, *f.,* fortune, the goddess Fortune* C21
frāter, frātris, *m.,* brother
fugiō, -ere, fūgī, ——, to flee, run away* C10
fūmus, -ī, *m.,* smoke* C16
fūnestus, -a, -um, *adj.,* deadly* C16
fūr, fūris, *m.,* thief* C20
fūrtum, -ī, *n.,* theft* C20
futūrus, -a, -um, *participle,* about to be* C21

G

Gallī, -ōrum, *m. pl.,* the Gauls, the inhabitants of France
gaudium, -ī, *n.,* joy
gaudium, -ī, *n.,* joy* C5
gerō, -ere, gessī, gestum, to carry; **sē gerit,** s/he behaves C9; *with clothing or articles of clothing as its object,* to wear; **bellum gerere,** to wage war* C12
gladius, -ī, *m.,* sword* C14
Graecia, -ae, *f.,* Greece
Graecus, -a, -um, *adj.,* Greek; **Graecī, -ōrum,** *m. pl.,* the Greeks
gremium, -ī, *n.,* bosom, lap* C7
gutta, -ae, *f.,* drop

H

habeō, -ēre, habuī, habitum, to have* C2
habitō (1), to live, dwell* C2
hāc nocte, tonight
herba, -ae, *f.,* plant, vegetation* C19
heus!, hey!
hic, haec, hoc, *demonstrative pronoun and adj.,* this, latter* C19
homō, -inis, *m.,* man (i.e., human being); *pl.* people* C8
honor, -ōris, *m.,* honor, public office or distinction* C21
hostis, -is, *m.,* enemy* C10
hūc atque illūc, hither and thither, to and fro
hūmānus, -a, -um, *adj.,* human* C20
Hūnī, -ōrum, *m. pl.,* the Huns

I

iaceō, -ēre, iacuī, ——, to lie down, be inert* C6
iaciō, -ere, iēcī, iactum, to throw* C17
iam, *adv.,* already* C14
iānua, -ae, *f.,* door
ibi, *adv.,* there* C12
igitur, *conj.,* therefore* C16
ignis, -is, *m.,* fire* C12
ille, illa, illud, *demonstrative pronoun and adj.,* that, former* C20
illūc, *adv.,* to that place, thither
imparātus, -a, -um, *adj.,* unprepared

impedimentum, -ī, *n.,* impediment
imperātor, -ōris, *m.,* emperor* C17
impetus, -ūs, *m.,* impetus, force, attack* C17
importūnus, -a, -um, *adj.,* boorish
improbus, -a, -um, *adj.,* bad, wicked
in, *prep. + abl.,* in, on* C3
in, *prep. + acc.,* into, to* C4
incendium, -ī, *n.,* conflagration, eruption* C16
industria, -ae, *f.,* industry, care
inīquitās, -ātis, *f.,* injustice* C20
inīquus, -a, -um, *adj.,* unjust
initium, -ī, *n.,* beginning* C17
inquam, I say/I said (*only introducing direct speech*)* C15
inquit, s/he says or said (*only introducing direct speech*)* C12
intellegō, -ere, intellēxī, intellēctum, to understand* C8
inter, *prep. + acc.,* between, among* C19
intereā, *adv.,* meanwhile
intrō (1), to enter* C4
inūsitātus, -a, -um, *adj.,* strange, unusual
invideō, -ēre, invīdī, invīsum + *dat.,* to envy someone* C7
invīsō, -ere, invīsī, invīsum, to visit
ipse, ipsa, ipsum, *demonstrative pronoun and adj.,* -self
īra, -ae, *f.,* anger* C12
is, ea, id, *personal and demonstrative pronoun and adj.,* s/he/it, this, that* C12
ita, *adv.,* so, in such a way C18; yes* C11
Ītalia, -ae, *f.,* Italy
itaque, *conj.,* and so* C1
iubeō, -ēre, iussī, iussum + *acc. + inf.,* to order somebody to do something* C4
iudex, -icis, *m.,* judge* C13
iūdicō (1), to judge* C6
Iuppiter, Iovis, *m.,* Jupiter, king of gods (in Greek, Zeus)
iussus, -ūs, *m.,* order (*usually employed in the ablative singular only*)* C17
iūstus, -a, -um, *adj.,* legitimate, just* C4

L
lacrima, -ae, *f.,* tear* C5
laqueus, -ī, *m.,* noose, lasso
leaena, -ae, *f.,* lioness
legō, -ere, lēgī, lēctum, to read, choose* C16
lēx, lēgis, *f.,* law* C20
liber, librī, *m.,* book* C6
līberō (1) + *acc. + abl.,* to free someone from something* C8
licet + *dat. + inf.,* it is allowed, it is permitted for someone to do something* C13
ligneus, -a, -um, *adj.,* wooden
littera, -ae, *f.,* letter of the alphabet; **litterae, -ārum,** *f. pl.,* literature, letter (epistle)* C6
lītus, -oris, *n.,* shore* C16
locus, -ī, *m.,* place; **locī, -ōrum,** *m. pl.,* passages of a book; **loca, -ōrum,** *n. pl.,* geographical places* C17
longē, *adv.,* far* C5
longus, -a, -um, *adj.,* long* C5
Lūcīlius, -ī, *m.,* Lucilius, a friend of Seneca's to whom he addressed his philosophical essays in the form of letters
lūculentus, -a, -um, *adj.,* splendid
lūdō, -ere, lūsī, lūsum, to play* C20
lūmen, -inis, *n.,* light
lupa, -ae, *f.,* she-wolf* C1

M
Maecēnās, Maecēnātis, *m.,* Maecenas, friend of Augustus, patron of the arts
māgnus, -a, -um, *adj.,* large, great, important* C4
māiōrem, *adj.* (*accusative singular feminine*), bigger, greater
male, *adv.,* badly
malitia, -ae, *f.,* badness, wickedness
malus, -a, -um, *adj.,* bad* C4
maneō, -ēre, mānsī, mānsum, to remain* C6
manus, -ūs, *f.,* hand* C17
Mārcus Tullius Cicero, -ōnis, *m.,* Marcus Tullius Cicero
mare, maris, *n.,* sea* C9
marītus, -ī, *m.,* husband* C18
Mārs, -tis, Mars, the god of war (in Greek, Ares)
māter, mātris, *f.,* mother* C16
mēcum = cum mē, with me* C13
mellītus, -a, -um, *adj.,* sweet as honey
memoria, -ae, *f.,* memory* C6
mercimōnium, -ī, *n.,* merchandise
Mercurius, -ī, *m.,* Mercury, messenger god, patron of merchants, travelers, thieves (in Greek, Hermes)
merīdiēs, -ēī, *m.,* midday* C18
meus, -a, -um, *possessive adj.,* my* C7
mīles, -itis, *m.,* soldier* C8
minimē, *adv.,* no* C11
Mīsēnum, -ī, *n.,* a base for the imperial Roman navy in the Bay of Naples; **Mīsēnī,** at Misenum
miser, misera, miserum, *adj.,* wretched* C5
mittō, -ere, mīsī, missum, to send* C11
mōns, montis, *m.,* mountain* C16
mordeō, -ēre, momordī, morsum, to bite
mors, mortis, *f.,* death* C9
mortuus, -a, -um, *adj.,* dead
moveō, -ēre, mōvī, mōtum, to move* C10
mox, *adv.,* soon* C14
Mūcius (-ī) Scaevola (-ae), *m.,* Mucius Scaevola
mulier, -ieris, *f.,* woman* C9
multum, *adv.,* much* C18
multus, -a, -um, *adj.,* much, many* C6
mūnimentum, -ī, *n.,* protection, fortification
mūrus, -ī, *m.,* wall, wall-fence* C17
mūtō (1), to change* C21

N
nam, *conj.,* for, in fact* C5
nārrō (1), to tell* C2
nauta, -ae, *m.,* sailor* C1
nāvigō (1), to sail, voyage* C8
nāvis, -is, *f.,* ship* C16
-ne, a particle added to the first word of an interrogative sentence* C11
nec, *conj.,* and not, nor* C10
necō (1), to kill
neglegō, -ere, neglēxī, neglēctum, to neglect* C15
nēminī, to nobody

Nerō, Nerōnis, *m.,* Nero, Julio-Claudian emperor
nihil, *negative pronoun,* nothing* C13
nisi, *conj.,* if not, unless
nōbīscum = cum nōbīs
noctū, *adv.,* during the night* C20
nōlō, *irregular verb,* not to want, be unwilling
nōlō, *irregular verb,* not to want, be unwilling* C13
nōmen, -inis, *n.,* name* C12
nōn sōlum . . . , sed etiam . . . , not only . . . , but also . . .*C5
nōn, *negative adv.,* not* C2
nōnne?, don't you?
nōs, *personal pronoun,* we* C12
noster, nostra, nostrum, *possessive adj.,* our* C12
nōtus, -a, -um, *adj.,* known
novus, -a, -um, *adj.,* new* C11
nox, noctis, *f.,* night* C10
nūbēs, -is, *f.,* cloud* C16
nūgae, -ārum, *f. pl.,* trifles
num?, do I? (negative answer implied)
numquam, *adv.,* never* C16
nunc, *adv.,* now* C2

O

ō, *interjection,* oh!
occīdō, -ere, occīdī, occīsum, to kill
occīdō, -ere, occīdī, occīsum, to kill* C12
occultātus, -a, -um, *adj.,* hidden
occultō (1), to hide* C18
occultus, -a, -um, *adj.,* hidden
oculus, -ī, *m.,* eye* C7
odium, -ī, *n.,* hatred* C14
oleum, -ī, *n.,* oil
omnis, -e, *adj.,* each, every, all* C13
opprimō, -ere, oppressī, oppressum, to overwhelm, suppress* C16
oppugnō (1), to attack
ōrāculum, -ī, *n.,* oracle* C8
ōrātiō, -ōnis, *f.,* speech; **ōrātiōnem habēre,** to make a speech* C9
ōs, ōris, *n.,* mouth* C14
ostendō, -ere, ostendī, ostentum, to show* C12

P

paene, *adv.,* almost* C20
papae!, wow!
parātus, -a, -um, *adj.,* prepared (often + *inf.*)
parēns, -rentis, *m./f.,* parent* C14
pariēs, parietis, *m.,* wall
parō (1), to prepare, get ready C2, design* C5
pars, partis, *f.,* part* C16
parvus, -a, -um, *adj.,* small* C15
passer, -eris, *m.,* sparrow* C7
pater, -tris, *m.,* father* C18
patria, -ae, *f.,* fatherland* C2
paucī, -ae, -a, *adj.,* few* C10
paulisper, *adv.,* for a little while
pauper, pauperis, *adj.,* poor* C20
pāx, pācis, *f.,* peace* C7
pectus, -oris, *n.,* chest* C14
pellis, -is, *f.,* skin, hide* C19
per, *prep. + acc.,* through* C14
perīculum, -ī, *n.,* danger* C10
permoveō, -ēre, -mōvī, -mōtum, to perturb
Persae, -ārum, *m. pl.,* the Persians
petō, -ere, petīvī, petītum, to seek, head for, go to* C8
piger, pigra, pigrum, *adj.,* lazy
pīpiō, -āre, ——, ——, to chirp
pirum, -ī, *n.,* pear (fruit)
pirus, -ī, *f.,* pear tree
plēnus, -a, -um, *adj. + gen. or + abl.,* full of* C20
pluit, -ere, pluit, ——, *an impersonal verb (used only in 3rd sg.),* to rain
plūs quam, more than
poena, -ae, *f.,* punishment
poēta, -ae, *m.,* poet* C1
pōmum, -ī, *n.,* fruit* C20
pōnō, -ere, posuī, positum, to put, place* C12
porcus, -ī, *m.,* pig
porta, -ae, *f.,* gate
possideō, -ēre, possēdī, possessum, to possess* C21
possum, posse, potuī, ——, to be able, can* C6
post, *prep. + acc.,* after* C18
posteā, *adv.,* afterwards

posteā, *adv.,* afterwards* C1
postquam, *conj.,* after* C19
praeclārus, -a, -um, *adj.,* famous, distinguished* C4
praefectus, -ī, *m.,* prefect, commander, chief
praemium, -ī, *n.,* reward* C4
prīmum, *adv.,* first
prīmus, -a, -um, *adj.,* first* C14
prō certō, *adverbial phrase,* for certain, for sure* C21
prō Iuppiter!, by Jove!
prō, *prep. + abl.,* for, on behalf of* C13
proelium, -ī, *n.,* battle, combat* C19
profuga, -ae, *m.,* deserter
prope, *prep. + acc.,* near* C12
propter, *prep. + acc.,* because of, on account of* C6
Psȳchē (gen. Psȳchēs, dat. Psȳchē, acc. Psȳchēn, abl. Psȳchē), Psyche
puella, -ae, *f.,* girl* C1
puer, puerī, *m.,* boy* C3
pugnō (1), to fight* C10
pulcher, pulchra, pulchrum, *adj.,* beautiful, nice* C5
pulchritūdō, pulchritūdinis, *f.,* beauty
pūniō, -īre, pūnīvī, pūnītum, to punish* C20
putō (1), to think, consider* C7
Pȳramus, -ī, *m.,* Pyramus
Pyrrhus, -ī, *m.,* Pyrrhus, king of Epirus
Pȳthia, -ae, *f.,* the Pythian priestess, responsible for uttering the ambiguous oracles at the shrine of Apollo at Delphi, Greece

Q

quaerō, -ere, quaesīvī, quaesītum, to look for, search* C18
-que, *conj.,* and* C11
quī, quae, quod, *relative pronoun,* which, who, that* C14
quī, quae, quod?, *interrogative adjective,* which? what? * C15
quid agis, how are you?
quis, quid?, *interrogative pronoun,* who? what? * C13
quō?, to what place?

quōcum = cum quō, with whom
quōmodo, how?
quondam, *adv.*, once
quoque, *adv.*, also* C11

R

rādīx, rādīcis, *f.*, root
rāmus, -ī, *m.*, branch
recipiō, -ere, -cēpī, -ceptum, to take back* C21
rēgīna, -ae, *f.*, queen* C11
relinquō, -ere, relīquī, relictum, to leave behind, abandon* C11
Remus, -ī, *m.*, Remus, brother of Romulus
reparō (1), to repair
reprehendō, -ere, -prehendī, -prehēnsum, to blame, rebuke* C21
rēs, reī, *f.*, thing, matter* C18
respondeō, -ēre, -spondī, -spōnsum, to answer* C13
revēniō, -īre, -vēnī, -ventum, to return
rēx, rēgis, *m.*, king
rēx, rēgis, *m.*, king* C8
Rhēa Silvia, Rhēae Silviae, *f.*, Rhea Silvia, vestal virgins
rīvus, -ī, *m.*, brook, stream* C3
rogō (1), to ask* C13
Rōma, -ae, *f.*, Rome* C1
Rōmānus, -a, -um, *adj.*, Roman
Rōmānus, -a, -um, *adj.*, Roman* C4
Rōmulus, -ī, *m.*, Romulus, legendary founder of Rome
rota, -ae, *f.*, wheel* C21
ruber, rubra, rubrum, *adj.*, red* C14
rūsticus, -a, -um, *adj.*, rural, rustic* C15

S

sacer, sacra, sacrum, *adj.*, holy, sacred
sacra, -ōrum, *n. pl.*, religious rites
saepe, *adv.*, often* C6
sagitta, -ae, *f.*, arrow
salūtem plūrimam dīcit + *dat.*, s/he greets (someone) (a standard formula for beginning a letter). Literally it means "(s/he) says (i.e., wishes) very much health (the best of health) to . . ."
salvē!, hello!
sanguis, sanguinis, *m.*, blood* C14

sānō (1), to heal* C19
saxum, -ī, *n.*, stone, rock* C15
scientia, -ae, *f.*, knowledge
sciō, scīre, scīvī, scītum, to know* C9
sē, *acc. of the reflexive pronoun*, herself, himself, itself, themselves* C7
sed, *conj.*, but* C4
sedeō, -ēre, sēdī, sessum, to sit* C19
sella, -ae, *f.*, seat, chair
sēmoveō, -ēre, sēmōvī, sēmōtum, to remove
semper, *adv.*, always* C5
Seneca, -ae, *m.*, Seneca, Roman author
senectūs, -ūtis, *f.*, old age* C15
senex, -is, *m.*, old man* C7
sentiō, -īre, sēnsī, sēnsum, to feel* C9
sēparō (1), to separate* C14
servō (1), to save, preserve*
sevērus, -a, -um, *adj.*, serious, strict, severe C7*
sī, *conj.*, if* C18
sīcut, *adv.*, as
sīcut, *adv.*, just as* C15
silva, -ae, *f.*, forest* C11
similis, -e, *adj.* + *gen.* or + *dat.*, like, similar* C12
sine, *prep.* + *abl.*, without* C17
soleō, -ēre, solitus sum + *inf.*, to be accustomed* C6
sōlus, -a, -um, *adj.*, sole, only
somnus, -ī, *m.*, sleep* C18
soror, -ōris, *f.*, sister* C7
spectō (1), to look at, gaze, stare at
spēlunca, -ae, *f.*, cave* C11
statim, *adv.*, immediately* C12
stō, -āre, stetī, statum, to stand* C15
studeō, -ēre, studuī, —— + *dat.*, to study, be eager for, be interested in* C16
studiōsus, -a, -um, *adj.* + *gen.*, interested in, a student of
subitō, *adv.*, suddenly*
sum, esse, fuī, ——, to be* C6
summus, -a, -um, *adj.*, the top of
suus, -a, -um, *possessive adj.*, his, her, its, their* C13
Syrācūsānus, -a, -um, *adj.*, from Syracuse

T

taberna, -ae, *f.*, shop
tam, *adv.*, so* C18
tamen, *conj.*, however* C5
tandem, *adv.*, at last* C8
tangō, -ere, tetigī, tāctum, to touch* C14
tantum, *adv.*, only* C13
tantus, -a, -um, *adj.*, so great* C12
tēcum = cum tē, with you* C13
tempestās, -ātis, *f.*, storm* C11
templum, -ī, *n.*, temple* C8
temptō (1), to try* C17
tempus, -oris, *n.*, time* C9
tenebrae, -ārum, *f. pl.*, shadows, darkness* C6
teneō, -ēre, tenuī, tentum, to hold* C2
Terentia, -ae, *f.*, Terentia, wife of Cicero
terō, -ere, trīvī, trītum, to wear out, rub* C19
terra, -ae, *f.*, land* C1
terribilis, -e, *adj.*, terrifying* C19
tertius, -a, -um, *adj.*, third
Themistoclēs, Themistoclis, *m.*, Themistocles, Athenian general
Thisbē, Thisbēs (gen.), Thisbē (dat.), Thisbēn (acc.), Thisbē (voc.), *f.*, Thisbe
timeō, -ēre, timuī, ——, to fear, be afraid* C3
timor, -ōris, *m.*, fear* C8
tolerō (1), to tolerate, bear
tollō, -ere, sustulī, sublātum, to lift up, raise, destroy* C21
tonō, -āre, -uī, ——, to thunder
tōtus, -a, -um, *adj.*, whole
trāns Tiberim, on the other side of the Tiber river
trēs, tria, *numeral*, three
trīstitia, -ae, *f.*, sadness
Trōia, -ae, *f.*, Troy
Trōiānus, -a, -um, *adj.*, Trojan
tū, *personal pronoun*, you (sg.) * C3
tum, *adv.*, then* C13
tumultus, -ūs, *m.*, uproar, confusion* C17
tunc, *adv.*, then* C8
tuus, -a, -um, *possessive adj.*, yours, your (sg.) * C12

U

ubi, *adv.,* where
ubīque, *adv.,* everywhere* C15
Ulixes, Ulixis, *m.,* Odysseus, Ulysses (Latin)
ūllus, -a, -um, *adj.,* any* C21
umquam, *adv.,* ever* C15
ūnā, *adv.,* together* C11
ūnusquisque nostrum, each one of us
urbs, urbis, *f.,* city (usually the city of Rome) * C9
uxor, -ōris, *f.,* wife* C18

V

valdē, *adv.,* very, exceedingly* C3
valē!, goodbye!* C13
vectus, -a, -um, *adj.,* carried, driven
vēlāmen, vēlāminis, *n.,* veil
venēnum, -ī, *n.,* poison* C4
veniō, -īre, vēnī, ventum, to come* C9
ventus, -ī, *m.,* wind* C17
Venus, Veneris, *f.,* Venus, goddess of beauty and love (in Greek, Aphrodite)
verbum, -ī, *n.,* word* C7
versō (1), to turn* C21
vērus, -a, -um, *adj.,* true* C15
Vesta, -ae, *f.,* Vesta, goddess of the hearth (in Greek, Hestia)
vester, vestra, vestrum, *possessive adj.,* yours (pl.), your* C12
vestīmentum, -ī, *n.,* garment, (pl.) clothes* C19
Vesuvius, -ī, *m.,* (Mount) Vesuvius
vetustus, -a, -um, *adj.,* old* C15
Via Sacra, a street in the Roman Forum
via, -ae, *f.,* road* C3
victōria, -ae, *f.,* victory
videō, -ēre, vīdī, vīsum, to see, (passive) seem* C2
vīlicus, -ī, *m.,* bailiff, steward
vīlla, -ae, *f.,* country house, villa* C15
vincō, -ere, vīcī, victum, to conquer, defeat* C8
vīnctus, -a, -um, *adj.,* bound, chained
vinculum, -ī, *n.,* chain, fetter* C4
vir, virī, *m.,* man* C3
vīs, ——, *f., pl.* **vīrēs, vīrium,** force, strength; **prō vīribus,** with all one's might* C12
vīta, -ae, *f.,* life* C6
vīvō, -ere, vīxī, vīctum, to live* C19
vocō (1), to call* C2
vōs, *personal pronoun,* you (pl.) * C12
vulnerō (1), to wound* C19
vulnus, -eris, *n.,* wound* C19
vult, he wishes
Xerxēs, Xerxis, *m.,* Xerxes, the great king of the Persians (who invaded Greece in 480 BCE)

PHOTOGRAPHY CREDITS

CHAPTER 1
Mars (© 2008 Jupiter Images Corp.)
Romulus and Remus Coin (© 2008 Shutterstock Images LLC)

CHAPTER 2
Greek Actor in a Mask (© 2008 Jupiter Images Corp.)
Roman Theatre in Mérida (© 2008 Shutterstock Images LLC)

CHAPTER 3
Actors in a Play (© 2008 Jupiter Images Corp.)
The Wolf and Lamb (© 2008 Jupiter Images Corp.)
Greek Mask (© 2008 Jupiter Images Corp.)

CHAPTER 4
Soldiers (© 2008 Jupiter Images Corp.)
Roman Leg Armor (© 2008 Jupiter Images Corp.)

CHAPTER 5
State of Kansas Seal (© 2008 Vector Images)
Statue of a Woman and Baby (© 2008 Jupiter Images Corp.)

CHAPTER 6
Children in School (© 2008 Jupiter Images Corp.)
Bust of Julius Caesar (© 2008 Jupiter Images Corp.)

CHAPTER 7
Mosaic of Pheasants (© 2008 Shutterstock Images LLC)
Romans in a Dining Room (© 2008 Jupiter Images Corp.)

CHAPTER 8
Xerxes with his Servants (© 2008 Jupiter Images Corp.)
Treasury at Delphi (© 2008 Shutterstock Images LLC)

CHAPTER 9
Rome Personified on a Republican Coin (© 2008 Shutterstock Images LLC)
Catilinarian Conspiracy (© 2008 Jupiter Images Corp.)

CHAPTER 10
Laocoön Sculpture (© 2008 Shutterstock Images LLC)
Ruins at Troy (© 2008 Jupiter Images Corp.)

CHAPTER 11
Dido and Aeneas (© 2008 Jupiter Images Corp.)
Dido Fresco (© 2008 Jupiter Images Corp.)

CHAPTER 12
Mucius and fire (© 2008 Jupiter Images Corp.)
Etruscan Breastplate (© 2008 Jupiter Images Corp.)

CHAPTER 13
Roman Shield (© 2008 Jupiter Images Corp.)
Via Sacra (© 2008 Shutterstock Images LLC)

CHAPTER 14
Thisbe at the Wall (© 2008 Jupiter Images Corp.)
Ovid (© 2008 Jupiter Images Corp.)

CHAPTER 15
Seneca in the Bathtub (© 2008 Jupiter Images Corp.)
Villa of Diomedes (© 2008 Jupiter Images Corp.)
Tomb of Seneca (© 2008 Jupiter Images Corp.)

CHAPTER 16
Roman Ship (© 2008 Jupiter Images Corp.)
Cave Canem Mosaic (© 2008 Jupiter Images Corp.)
Skull Mosaic (© 2008 Shutterstock Images LLC)

CHAPTER 17
Assassination of Julius Caesar (© 2008 Jupiter Images Corp.)
Bust of Tiberius (© 2008 Jupiter Images Corp.)
Caligula (© 2008 Jupiter Images Corp.)

CHAPTER 18
Roman banquet (© 2008 Jupiter Images Corp.)
Pompeiian Amphoras (© 2008 Jupiter Images Corp.)

CHAPTER 19
Huns on the March (© 2008 Jupiter Images Corp.)
Attila and the Huns (© 2008 Jupiter Images Corp.)
Attila the Hun (© 2008 Jupiter Images Corp.)

CHAPTER 20
St. Augustine (© 2008 Jupiter Images Corp.)
Dido and Aeneas (© 2008 Jupiter Images Corp.)

CHAPTER 21
Boethius (© 2008 Jupiter Images Corp.)

Made in the USA
Monee, IL
16 December 2019